Ben Kimpel

Susan Wade Wink

THE MUDGE PRESS

PREFACE

When the Porter Fund asked me to write this biography, I accepted the honor without hesitation but not without reservation. To write about Ben Kimpel seemed to me at once the most delightful and the most daunting of tasks; on the side of delight was the opportunity to be with him again, to spend long hours in his company through the agency of my own memory as well as the memories of others. Having the pleasure of such reverie sanctioned by commission would have seemed to me almost sinful had I not realized from the beginning that it would also be painful; the sense of loss, the helpless longing to have him back washed over me with each return from the sessions of sweet silent thought to present reality. That while absorbed by the work I felt him alive undoubtedly prolonged the making of this book.

The chance to discover something more about his life was also inviting. I suppose most of his students at one time or another have wanted to know more about the events, the people, and the experiences that helped to shape the man they so admired; to have that sort of curiosity about one's heroes is natural. It is also natural, in the absence of an abundance of clear facts about a hero, for legends to emerge, develop, and accrue to his name, and because the legends, too, reflect a kind of truth, they soon become such an integral part of the image that the points at which they are grafted to the facts that give them life become very difficult to find. The challenge of trying to find those points appealed to me.

What was daunting about undertaking to write a biography of Ben Kimpel should be rather obvious. Surely, no one but a fool or a supreme egoist could imagine herself adequately qualified to record the life of one whose . learning, whose interests, whose character, and whose humanity were as great as Ben Kimpel's. I questioned the wisdom of attempting to capture even a small portion of his greatness of mind and of spirit; and, readily admitting my inadequacies, I asked myself if I had any qualifications at all for such an attempt.

Between 1967 and 1973, I took twenty-four hours of coursework for my M.A. and Ph.D. from Ben. During those years I and my fellows were often in his company at parties, and he occasionally came to my home for lunch or dinner. After my husband, Johnny, and I left Fayetteville in 1973, Johnny and Ben began to correspond, and a friendship developed that lasted the rest of Ben's life. Among the many incomparable rewards of this friendship were numerous week-end visits in Ben's home or ours, in Little Rock or some other appointed meeting place in the state, and four ten-day to two-week spring or summer trips to the west--three of them in Ben's car—and I was along on all but one.

Thus, insofar as the time we spend in one's presence qualifies us to comment on his life, I can offer the following credentials: over 1000 hours in Ben's classroom, about 180 hours in a car with him, at least 300 hours with him at tables in bars and restaurants scattered across twelve states and two countries, 200 or so hours as a guest in his home, 200 or so more as his host in mine, some 100 hours sitting around hotel rooms, and another 200 plus walking around canyons, mountains, cities, ruins, and deserts with him. Something over 2100 hours is not many—certainly not as many as I wanted and still want to spend in Ben's company—but they are quality hours every one, lived and remembered vividly. One of the things that has struck me most in the months I have been working on this book is how clear and lively everyone's memories of Ben are. Years after his death, people continue to speak of him with an immediacy that suggests that he is still just down the hall or sitting under his floodlight reading lamp on Rock Street studying Chinese or perhaps travelling abroad again. This clarity is partly the result of Ben's having been clear and direct and vivid himself, but mainly, I think, the memories draw their vitality from the simple fact that he was just great fun to be with, in or out of the classroom.

Returning to the question of qualification, I also shared many of his interests and tastes, although certainly his appreciation for literature, music, good food, good wines, travel, mountains, wildflowers, languages, wit, and cheeseburgers was deeper than mine because of his superior knowledge and superior
capacities—mental, spiritual, and physical.

But any attempt to make myself feel qualified for my task was bound to end in failure. I looked instead for reasons why I should presume to write a biography of Ben.

First of all, a book that includes anecdotes, what some refer to as "Ben stories," would be sure to give a good deal of pleasure to anyone who knew him and, very likely, to many who did not. I've never known anyone who knew him who did not enjoy exchanging these stories, yet, to my knowledge, few if any of them have been recorded. It seemed to need doing, and so one motivation for my undertaking to do it was that no one else had.

Secondly, my belief that the example of so good a life as Ben's can continue to influence the world for the better was an incentive to do what I could to perpetuate his memory. In the course of one interview, someone remarked, with reference to Ben's lack of any sense of self-importance, that he would not have wanted his biography to be written. At the time the comment impressed me as undeniably true, but, upon reflection, I realized that if we had only recorded the lives of those who wanted their lives recorded, we would still have biographies aplenty of some very great men and women, but we would have no record of those very great men and women who happened also to be humble, and, insofar as biographies may give us models to which we might do well to aspire, that would be a misfortune indeed.

Furthermore, perhaps rather than his not wanting a biography, he simply could not have understood or imagined why anyone would want it. I doubt that the idea would even have occurred to him. He used to say that it bored him to talk about himself, and, opinions that he was "an extremely private person" aside, that may be the whole truth. Two things about his character may have conspired to make rehearsing his own life a tedious business for him: his humility, which would make it seem to him tedious for others, and his love of learning, which, because he already knew it and therefore couldn't be learning anything while he was talking about it, made it tedious for him.

For most students—at least, for most in the English graduate program—Ben Kimpel's reputation preceded him into the classroom, sometimes by hours or days, sometimes by years. Rarely did a student encounter him in class for the first time without already having heard a good many tales of this phenomenal teacher. Former students who had become teachers themselves sent their favorite students, who were generally also their best, to study under Ben, and they, along with those who simply happened into his courses, yearly swelled the ranks of the devoted.

Ben was by no means unique in having such a following; in the late sixties at least, virtually all of the professors in the University of Arkansas English department, which included the MFA program for writers, had their ardent disciples. And the forms of devotion were similar in most ways: taking as many courses from the professors as possible, seeking their company socially, and telling and exchanging anecdotes about them.

It was through the last of these forms of devotion that new graduate students usually received their introduction to Ben Kimpel. "Kimpel" was one of the first names I heard when I arrived in Fayetteville in the fall of 1967 to begin graduate study, and the context in which I first heard it is probably commonplace in the history of students' admiration for their teachers. A graduate student who occupied with her husband the other half of the duplex where I was living pronounced the name often in a variety of tones from beseeching and loving to reproving. She was addressing her cat, a huge, yellow tiger-striped tom whom she had named for her favorite professor. It was some years before I was in a position to appreciate the irony of this particular tribute to Ben.

He was not fond of cats, which, being a cat lover myself, I considered one of the few serious flaws in his character. Although he was quite tolerant of and even kind to the cats that belonged to his friends (he sat for many hours stroking Jessie O'Kelly's big, friendly

Siamese cat and several different cats in our home over the years, all of them attracted to his ample lap and gentle touch), he kept a pan of water handy to throw on the cats that came begging at his door on Rock Street, and once when several of us were taking breakfast with him at his massive medieval dining table, one small black cat appeared at the front window and another at the back. Johnny, who was a master at baiting Ben and leading him into discussions or games that invariably resulted in pronouncements either witty or profound or, very often, both, began to badger Ben about his distaste for cats. Finally Ben allowed that in fact he liked cats all right in the abstract.

"Well, what about that one? It looks pretty abstract," Johnny said, indicating the one at the back window that was looking for all the world like an Egyptian statuette.

Ben glanced at it over his shoulder, turned quickly back to his scrambled eggs, and, shaking his head, grumbled, "It's not quite abstract enough."

The student who gave her cat Ben's name was always a little afraid that he would find out, but since she was kept at a distance—largely, perhaps, by the very force of her admiration—from someone she respected and loved, she fulfilled at least a bit of her desire to be close to him by assuring that she might say his name frequently with complete ease and familiarity. And such is the nature of adoration that it often manifests itself in ways that would strike the adored as altogether inappropriate—and even a little silly.

And so it may be with this book. If Ben knows of this endeavor, may he forgive us our desire to know as much about him as we can discover; I think he surely will.

Wanting to share the pleasures of knowing Ben and to capture in some measure the great example of his life contributed to my willingness to attempt this book, but finally one reason would have sufficed: I loved him. Hundreds, perhaps thousands, of others loved him, too. This book is for them—for us.

In his fine book *Writing Lives: Principia Biographica*, Leon Edel maintains that "no good biography can be written in total love and admiration," and I must admit that the statement gave me pause. However, I preserved hope in two ways: first, by withholding a complete trust that Edel's pronouncement is the unqualified truth; and second, in case it is, by slipping through past the word "total." Certainly, my love and admiration of Ben Kimpel are about as great as I can imagine having for anyone, but "total" is an absolute word, and its use to describe something as nebulous and complex as human feeling seems dubious.

I accepted the commission for this biography with every intention of remaining thoroughly objective. I had to give that up. I cannot imagine that anyone who knew Ben could write a completely objective biography of him, so compelling was his character. It needs a disinterested party--someone who knew him only by reputation or not--to write the biography I cannot write. I have, however, been objective in my search for the facts of his life and for the views of others who knew him.

The search for facts was difficult, and much remains to be discovered. Ben was not a sentimental man, and, as a rule, he kept neither mementos nor letters; the letters he did save were unfortunately destroyed soon after his death. Most of what he kept had to do with his travels--staggering collections of maps, photographs, slides, brochures, tickets, and even luggage tags, from sixty years of travelling. Otherwise, his books and his records were all he held on to. He did not throw away his diploma from Chapel Hill, but it was found rolled up and crumpled in the bottom of a bureau drawer.

In my interviews in person and by mail with numbers of Ben's graciously cooperative family, former students, friends, colleagues, and acquaintances, I soon began to feel rather like some kind of reverse Diogenes: I had found the honest man and had then to search for his flaws. To those who suggested early on that this book would probably be little more than a "puff piece," to use their jargon, I would say that, although this biography is not objective, it is honest. Such flaws as others perceived or as I myself observed are here; I have included what I have known and discovered about the life and character of Ben Drew Kimpel, omitting nothing which I could substantiate. I really don't know what else I could have done.

The depth of my gratitude and the extent of my debt to those who have made this work possible cannot be expressed; I must be content with the hope that a few inadequate words of thanks to the following people will be understood as signifying. much, much more: to Jack Butler, Chairman, and Phil McMath, Secretary of the Porter Fund, for their trust and patience; to Mr. and Mrs. Charles Warner for their help in obtaining invaluable documents and photographs; to Edouard Desrochers, Assistant Librarian and Academy Archivist at Phillips Exeter Academy; to all of Ben's friends, colleagues, and former students whose names, memories, and words appear in the following pages and who are, in fact, the co-authors of this book--particularly Jessie O'Kelly, Juliet Eaves, Lyna Lee Montgomery, Claude Faulkner, Leo Van Scyoc, David Hart, Lyell Behr, Richard Marius, Brynhild Rowberg, Dr. Valentine Hagstrom, David Strain, Doug Howard, Claude Gibson, Russ Goodyear, Perry Dillon, Bill Meyer, and Rodolphus and Marie Whitten-for having, in some cases, affirmed the light and, in others, illuminated the darkness. I am also very grateful to all who read the manuscript through its numerous revisions—especially Juanita Sandford, whose suggestions were exceptionally helpful both because she is a careful and exacting reader and because, not having known Ben, she was able to approach the subject objectively. And finally, for their encouragement and patience, for the countless ways, large and small, that they helped me, and for their love, without which, I fear, I would accomplish nothing, I thank my husband, Johnny, and my son, Gene.

Preface

   Ben believed in accepting graciously tributes and awards given for achievements resulting from honest efforts. On his vita he cited only two: his election to Phi Beta Kappa and his receipt of the first Arkansas Alumni Teaching Award, which recognized the success of his efforts to be, respectively, a good student and a good teacher. I would like to think of this biography as a tribute to his apparently unceasing efforts to do something else really well--to live a good and honest life. He did that successfully, too. No one ever did it better. I am one of God knows how many people in whose lives and thought Ben Kimpel remains perhaps the single greatest influence. All of us cherish the attitudes, the knowledge, and the memories he gave us. So rich and various were his gifts that as many biographies could exist as there are people who knew him. I wish they could all be written. I hope they will be.

   Here is mine.

CHAPTER ONE

Even filled with people, the halls and classrooms echo—it's the wooden floors and the high plaster ceilings and all that space between them. The room is large but still rather crowded, and, in the warm September-afternoon air, smells of chalk-dust, new books, old books, sweat, perfumes, and sharpened pencils mingle together and blend into the permanent smell of the room: the redolence of decades of chalk-dust, new books, old books, sweat, perfumes, and sharpened pencils.

Most of the students are engaged in the animated conversation that so often accompanies beginnings, and scattered laughter adds to the atmosphere suggestions of reunion, camaraderie, and anticipation. A few people sit silent, self-consciously flipping through a textbook or absorbed in writing something or another; they are some of the first-year graduate students perhaps. It is the first day of classes.

Several minutes before the bell rings, a large man briskly enters the room, his arm curled around a bundle of books and papers. His thinning grey hair is neatly combed, and its having been very recently cut calls attention to his ears. Despite the uncomfortable warmth and the hour, he looks freshly scrubbed, an impression enhanced by the flushed fair skin.

One senses that the figure he cuts is somehow out of proportion: the arms too short, perhaps, for his height--an inch or two shy of six feet--or too small in relation to the massive, sloping shoulders and considerable girth at the waist-line. or maybe it is only that the way he wears his pants hitched up and belted above that girth makes the high waist appear to be even higher. Or it could be that the head is more delicately shaped than the bulk of the rest of his body-suggests it should be. And something else is vaguely incongruous: for all his size and mass, he moves lightly; his step has both a buoyancy and a kind of graceful grandeur, like a dancer's.

His brown trousers hit him about an inch above the laces of his dark brown cap-toe oxfords, and the plaid shirt looks fresh, as if it has just been pressed, although the collar is a little frayed and there's a hole in the sleeve an inch or so below the elbow.

The buzz of conversation hardly abates at all as he mounts the platform, which rises some six inches above the floor, and takes his chair. He seems a little nervous, mildly flustered, as he arranges the books and a scrap or two of paper on the desk before him. A few of the returning graduate students with whom he exchanged greetings when he came in asked about the trip from which he has recently returned or about his summer in general. He responds quietly and pleasantly, nodding his head as he speaks to indicate that he has found it all really quite satisfactory.

When the bell rings he has just taken the first puff of a cigarette drawn from his left shirt pocket with the thumb and forefinger of his right hand and lit it with a paper match. As soon as the bell sounds, he begins talking, and by the time the sound of the bell fades away his is the only voice to be heard in the room. Although his voice is clear and well-modulated, it is not particularly pleasing, somewhat flat and nasal; there is little if any trace of a regional accent to indicate his origins.

He outlines the business of the class first, goes over the thorough syllabus which has been distributed, and summarizes what will be covered and what will be expected from the students concerning tests and papers. He briefly describes the kinds of tests he gives, particularly the reading quizzes, and, the preliminaries out of the way, he plunges right into the backgrounds of the course. The scrap of paper which served to remind him of announcements and corrections of the reading list is stuck into a book; he proceeds with no notes at all. Dates, historical and literary facts, summaries of and images from dozens of works, commentary, answers to all questions--everything flows accurately and effortlessly from his memory.

Because his narrative, responses, and comments are so direct, he covers a great deal of material in what remains of the class period yet creates the illusion of moving along at a comfortable, even leisurely pace that is belied only by the furious rate at which the students must take notes to keep abreast of the flood of information. Most of the time, except for the necessity of writing very fast, note-taking is easy; he tends toward the epigrammatic, and responses to questions often begin with something like, "Well--two things about that . . . ." But for the student encountering him for the first time some problems arise: his tendency, for example, to stop mid-thought either to rephrase the idea or to offer a parenthetical explanation.

During the fifty minutes, he smokes almost constantly, usually fishing into the shirt pocket for another of the unfiltered Camels as he is grinding the previous one out on the floor beside his desk. He smokes in short, frequent puffs, the only mannerism suggestive of restless nervousness that lasts beyond the first few moments of his lecture, and flicks the ashes onto the floor beside him.

He raises his voice, lowers his chin, and lifts his glasses just high enough to see under them when he reads aloud from a text. If he needs to write on the board, which he rarely does, and cannot scoot the chair around a bit to reach it, he noisily pushes away from the desk and gets up. Otherwise he stays seated for the whole period.

The time passes quickly. The sound of the bell is surprising; it seems to be ringing much too soon, and several students glance at their watches in disbelief. He completes his sentence loudly enough to be heard over the bell and the shuffling of papers and feet, and the class is over.

"So that's Ben Kimpel. He doesn't look anything like I thought he would." One first-year graduate student who, like many others, had only heard of Ben Kimpel before the first class meeting, had conjured an image of him based upon the reports of his great learning and wide travels. "He's so cultured!" he had been told. He imagined a rather small man, dressed in heavy tweeds and sporting a neatly trimmed beard. When Ben appeared in the classroom, the student thought he was some flunky who had been sent in to say that Kimpel wasn't back from Europe and to give a few assignments. By the end of that first hour, Ben had won his respect, and he knew--even without the stories--that he had been in the presence of greatness.

Ben Kimpel joined the faculty of the University of Arkansas at Fayetteville as an Assistant Professor of English in the fall of 1952 and spent the next thirty-one years, except for a few semesters of leave, teaching, inspiring, astounding, and delighting thousands of students. Since he spent almost half of his sixty-seven years as a teacher, a majority of the people whose lives he touched were undoubtedly students; on the assumption, then, that a goodly number of my readers remember Ben primarily as a teacher, I have begun with what was for most of us the beginning, not only to rekindle the memories of those who were in his classes but also to introduce him to those who were not in something like the way his students first perceived him.

Unfortunately, no description can do more than approach the actual experience and can in no way substitute for it; it is one thing to remind someone who has seen and listened to Ben of, for example, some of his verbal habits--his fondness for the words 'clearly' and 'really' and for the phrase 'not altogether happy,' his pronunciation of 'at all,' the brusqueness of his 'What?' whenever someone spoke too softly for him to hear, the quizzical, tentative 'Well . ' that so often prefaced his response to a comment he found dubious--but it is quite another matter to create them for someone who never heard him.

However, there are actually two ways for those who never sat in Ben's classroom to get a better idea than words can provide of his style: first, the Department of English in Fayetteville has a collection of his lectures on video tape. Second, one might visit the classrooms of any number of his ex-students who have themselves become teachers; Ben will be there--in mannerisms, intonations, attitudes--in countless ways, large and small. One former student-become-teacher mystified his charges by periodically fumbling in his left shirt pocket; he was not even aware of this curious habit until someone who had been in one of his classes asked him about it. Only then did he realize that he was reaching for another cigarette. He had never been a smoker. In any gathering of Ben's former students one is likely to see imaginary jowls shaken or hear that emphatic 'at all.' His voice has persisted in the woods so long it probably never will be lost.

The qualities of a great teacher are as various and difficult to pinpoint as the qualities of a great book; just when you think you have the category neatly defined, along comes an example of greatness that simply will not fit. Ben spoke of the problems with determining whether someone is a good teacher or not in his C. W. Oxford lecture, given only months before his death. Discussing the three areas--teaching, service, and publication-- in which one is measured for a job, a promotion, or tenure, he maintained that, although everyone says that teaching is the most important of the three, the profession has not yet found a way to measure it: "There seems to be no way to demonstrate that X is a better teacher than Y; so everybody pays lip service to that area, but in point of fact you don't get much reward for it--unless you want your students to think well of you; they're the only people who really know actually whether you're any good or not." That one of the only two honors Ben listed on his vita was the Alumni Distinguished Faculty Award (the first, in 1961] suggests that he felt justifiable pride in having been adjudged 'good' by "the only people who really know."

Rather than create a list of criteria for a great teacher based upon the example of Ben Kimpel, let it suffice to say that Ben Kimpel was a great teacher, and here are some of his qualities and some things he did.

One of the first things people tend to bring up about Ben is the breadth of his learning. He knew a good deal about just about everything. In spite of his not subscribing to, much less reading, a daily newspaper, he generally knew more about what of any importance was going on in the world and where in the world it was going on than the most avid followers of the news. His knowledge of geography was phenomenal, for reasons that will become obvious; he had been everywhere. His command of languages is legendary, although he himself listed as the languages in which he was fluent only French and German; he read Old and Middle English, Italian, Latin, Greek, Provencal, Russian, Spanish, Old Icelandic, Chinese, and Japanese--some with the aid of a dictionary, most without--and Lyell Behr, who served with Ben for many years on the regional Woodrow Wilson Foundation scholarship committee--has told this anecdote:

> One evening we were having dinner in a place which had Egyptian hieroglyphics on either side of a doorway. He had said that he had taken a short course in hieroglyphics, so we asked him to translate. He did; one side was gibberish, and the other side, as I recall, had to do with a farmer's accounts.

He knew astronomy. On one of his trips to the southern hemisphere, he was having dinner at a terrace restaurant and overheard people at an adjoining table discussing the constellations. They were greatly confused. Ben politely offered to help them out and did so, charting for them all the constellations in the southern skies. He knew the religions of the world; however, he did write, before teaching one of his courses in world religions, "I wish I knew more about Islam"--hardly surprising—he wished to know more about almost everything.

If he had an academic area of weakness, it was the sciences. Lyell Behr has written regarding the interviews for the Woodrow Wilson fellowships, "I was the scientist of the group, and when we interviewed a candidate in the sciences--which was not often-Ben participated as he could. The second year he was able to ask these candidates good questions--he had spent time reading books in the sciences. He seemed to feel that his contribution was not great enough in the first year." One candidate in the sciences had a friend who was a graduate student at Fayetteville and called him after his unsuccessful interview. "Who's that fat guy?" he asked. His friend told him that Ben taught English. "English!" cried the hapless candidate, incredulous; "that guy teaches English?" He was certain that he had failed because of his inability to answer Ben's questions.

Because he considered them inseparable from literature, Ben knew world history and philosophy extremely well. And then, of course, there was literature.

Claude Faulkner, the chairman of the English department when Ben came to Fayetteville and for some twenty years thereafter, has said of Ben: "I really and truly believe that he knew more-in breadth and depth--about world literature than anybody else living." Faulkner estimated that Ben had taught "fifty or sixty" courses during his tenure at the University. In a tribute delivered at the memorial service held several days after Ben's death, Leo Van Scyoc gave a partial list of the courses Ben had taught only since 1973:

Old English, Beowulf, Chaucer, Germanic and Celtic Backgrounds for Medieval Lit, Romance Backgrounds for Medieval Lit, Renaissance, Drama to 1642, 17th Century, Milton, 18th Century, Survey of English Lit--both parts, Modern British Literature, 20th-Century Continental Literature, Modern World Drama, Contemporary World Drama, Contemporary British and American Novel, Translation Workshop, Continental Novel, The Search for Values in Humanistic Disciplines, Modern American Poetry, American Novel, Yeats, Pound, T. S. Eliot, Freshman Composition, Continental Romanticism, Continental Realism to Symbolism, the Literature of China and Japan, and the

Literature of the Near East. And that doesn't include all the special readings courses he gave to graduate students, undergraduate honors reading courses, tutorials . . . .

Another of his most popular courses was the James Joyce seminar; in the humanities, he also taught World Religions and Twentieth-Century Thought. Furthermore, he did not limit his teaching to the University campus: at the free university sponsored by the Unitarian Church in Fayetteville, he taught a number of courses on all manner of things, including literature, philosophy, and world religions.

It may be of some interest to note that he taught most of these courses at the same time that he was serving as department chairman, an onerous responsibility for him which, for all its demands on his time and energy, he never allowed to supersede his responsibilities as a teacher and a scholar. Or perhaps I should say he never let it interfere with the joy he took in being a teacher and a scholar. In his Oxford lecture, having urged graduate students in the humanities to do scholarship and publish while they are still in graduate school, he cited two rewards, jobs and satisfaction. Of the latter reward he had this to say:

> You do it because you want to do it. People think it's funny to say that virtue is its own reward. I don't know why that's funny; if it's not, what is its reward? If you don't get a kick out of your own activity--and by this I mean both learning and teaching--you're not going to have a very happy life of it. It *should* be its own reward . . Dr. Oxford was just pointing out that he felt he had not deserved this . because he had enjoyed it all so much. Well, I'm going to make a confession: so have I. If I absolutely had to—and I don't want this to get out--I would be willing to *pay* in order to be allowed to talk to a class about William Butler Yeats. It's a great pleasure. In my opinion, scholarship is also a great pleasure. At least it means that I am never condemned to ask myself, "What'll I do? Well, I guess I'll look at 'Dallas' or maybe I'll look at Johnny Carson." I'm not that desperate, and I think this is a great relief!

To most students it came as a real surprise that the subject of Ben's doctoral thesis was Melville, and, although he taught more courses in medieval than in American literature, it was also a revelation to discover that he had come to the University as a medievalist. One student had another sort of surprise: his last year in undergraduate school, he was a candidate for a Woodrow Wilson fellowship. Ben, as I have already mentioned, was a member of the selection committee for the region that included

Arkansas, Tennessee, Kentucky, and Mississippi. The candidate did a little homework on each of the people who would be questioning him and discovered the title of Ben's doctoral thesis. He concentrated his study on 19th-century American literature, assuming he then would be able to field anything this Ben Kimpel threw his way. He came out of the interview dazzled; Ben had thrown him everything from the Anglo-Saxon Chronicles to Ken Kesey, and there the forlorn candidate had stood with his 19th-century-American Literature glove. In some respects, it was not a happy day; but in others, it was one of the happiest of his life. He came to Fayetteville to study under the man who he felt was largely responsible for his failure to receive one of the fellowships.

The breadth of Ben's knowledge had much to do with his greatness as a teacher, for it enabled him to place every writer and every work into the largest possible context. His discussions were not limited by narrow considerations of time, or place, or language; he held and managed to convey literature and history in a universal, and I am tempted to say eternal, perspective. In fact, he taught, for some years, what is referred to as the "Survey of Surveys"--a course in which he began at the beginnings of western literature and worked his way right through to the present, described by one who took it as "absolutely invaluable-all of the observations and the ,..;hole sweep of literature." That sense of having "the whole sweep of literature" presented was characteristic of his other courses as well; his references to traditions and influences, his analogies and allusions fostered this broad view, so that no writer or work was ever considered in a vacuum. He did it all very casually, too, as if it were the most natural thing in the world to know all these things. For him, I think, it was.

But for all his knowledge, culture, and learning, he had almost nothing of the pedant in him. I never saw him be ostentatious; he seemed not even tempted, as so many learned people quite naturally are, to make an unsolicited show of his learning. He was not, however, averse to command performances. The scene at parties became a familiar one: Ben stolidly situated in a comfortable chair with a dozen or so students grouped around him instigating in one way or another a display of his wit and his wisdom. He did not, I suppose, actively seek the role of guru, but neither did he actively resist it; in fact, he seemed to enjoy it a great deal. He was a very humble man, but he had no false humility; he was astute enough to recognize and respect his own gifts and valued his role as a positive influence on those who admired him.

Oh, he could be pedantic. He was without peer at playing the pedant, but he was generally careful not to do so except in the company of people who he knew would realize that he was playing, and then he played the role flawlessly; with his learning he had the wherewithal to out-Herod Herod. Otherwise, what might be construed as pedantry was rare. One day a student made some disparaging remark about opera in general and Wagnerian opera in particular, and Ben, who was a great lover of opera, snapped at him: "No one," he said with irritation, "can consider himself educated who has not heard the Ring cycle."

When the curriculum was being overhauled during the establishment of the J. William Fulbright School of Arts and Sciences, Ben sat on a committee which was discussing language requirements for certain courses of study. Some of the members kept asking why a foreign language should be required, and, after a number of good reasons had failed to convince the skeptics, Ben declared, "Because anybody who can't read French is an oaf!"

Had he been pressed on these occasions, he would have admitted, albeit grudgingly I suspect, that at best he was only half serious. One of the things that most struck people about him was his humility, how easily he wore his great learning. Dolphus Whitten remembers Ben from Camp Robinson, where they were stationed together in 1942 and 1943: "He never made a point of his brilliance--he was very unassuming; you just knew that here was someone who was extraordinarily bright." Although he was known for asking a great deal of his students, especially where reading was concerned, the greatest demands he made were on himself. He did not expect everyone to know what he knew or even what he felt he ought to know. He really did sort of wish, though, that everyone wanted to know things as much as he did.

Learning accompanied by a flair for the dramatic can be very attractive, but that was not Ben's style; in and out of the classroom, he was without affectation. He was so very down-to-earth that students in his classes often felt that, in addition to being in the presence of immense knowledge and wit, they were in touch with an elemental good sense which provided a subdued excitement, a certain security, and a solid sense of well-being.

A glance at any of the excerpts from his lectures in the appendices will reveal the astonishing amount of ground Ben could cover in a fifty-minute period (actually most of the transcripts are from thirty-minute tapes). The efficiency with which he covered material in class extended to other aspects of his role as a teacher as well. For one thing, he was always prepared. He must have read some works hundreds of times, because he always reviewed and often re-read anything he was going to teach very shortly before he taught it, often the night before. Also, he positively spoiled his students with how soon he graded and returned papers. When he urged the teaching assistants to return papers to their students as quickly as possible, his argument carried much more weight with the assistants who were or had been his students because they knew how much his promptness meant to them. Unfortunately, few of us had the kind of discipline necessary to emulate Ben, although his example probably speeded things up considerably. And after twenty years, I, for one, still feel guilty if I keep a set of papers longer than a week.

Another quality that made Ben attractive was his good nature. Although he had a strong irritable streak in him, he kept it under control remarkably well unless he was ill. Illness was also one of the few things that could depress him, but he was rarely ill, even more rarely depressed, and, when he was, he usually managed to lose all signs of his depression as soon as he entered the classroom. The man did love to teach. Furthermore, he had found the secret of happiness: "As soon as you ask yourself, 'Am I happy?'" he said more than once, "you're going to think of all kinds of reasons why you're not. The moral of this? Don't ask."

One result of, or perhaps one of the reasons for, his amiable nature was an uncommon degree of patience, which manifested itself in the classroom in a number of ways. Despite his asking the simplest questions he could think of on his reading quizzes, he was always ready to come up with others if a student could not answer the first question but insisted he or she had read the assignment. I have heard Ben give as many as five alternate questions on a single work in an attempt to find something a student could answer, although usually if the second or third alternative failed, Ben would give the student a dubious look, and, nodding his head slightly, say, "I really think you ought to read that again."

His patience sometimes became a source of exasperation for students who felt that valuable time was being wasted when Ben politely allowed someone in the class to talk on and on. It was possible to take advantage of Ben in this way, but, happily, few students did so; however, one in a classroom was enough to irritate the others. Ben rarely considered a question irrelevant, or, at least, he rarely responded to one as if he did. The questions that clearly annoyed him were the lazy ones which students asked either just to be asking a question or because they had not read or had not been listening. In response to these, Ben could be very short. Lyell Behr's description of Ben's demeanor in the Woodrow Wilson interviews applies as well to Ben's manner in the classroom: "In most interviews, he was gentle Ben. But he had little time for smart alecks or sloppiness. On a couple of candidates who had some sort of condescending attitude (imagine) he descended like the Assyrian, and reduced them to hamburger."

He also enjoyed a good argument, but would bring a dead-end debate to an abrupt halt by saying with some irritation, "Well, you may be right about that," and returning directly to what he had been talking about when the argument ensued. The way he delivered the line made it quite clear that he did not for a minute believe that his adversary "might be right about that." He tended to argue--truly argue--only with those students whom he respected and knew well enough to be certain that they would not be hurt or intimidated as a result of his arguments. Although at informal gatherings Ben would occasionally bring the full force of his argumentative powers to bear against these students, he rarely did so in class. On those instances when he did, the student with whom he was arguing usually felt honored to have brought Ben out, albeit briefly, in, as it were, his full armor, but uninformed onlookers were sometimes visibly shocked by what they perceived as Ben's brutality.

The desire to be fair was one thing that made him patient, and another was an abhorrence of censorship in any form, including intimidation. As the supervisor of the second half of the freshman composition course, he cautioned the graduate teaching assistants against the temptation to assign a low grade to a paper because it contained opinions which the grader found odious. More generally, he warned of the threat to justice that personal antagonisms could pose. He told one of his advisees who had a strong aversion to a student in one of her sections, "If I dislike a student, I try to lean over backwards to give him more than he deserves for fear I might be prejudiced in the other direction. You might do well to do that."

In his zeal to be fair to students and in his generosity to them in other respects, he came nearer to erring, in the eyes of many of his friends and colleagues, than in any other aspect of his character. As someone put it, "He wanted to give everyone the last chance, and sometimes, I think, he didn't see that in being kinder than he should have been to one student, maybe he was a bit unfair on the other hand to students who hadn't asked for any special favors." But it was particularly in respect to admitting to the graduate program people who, in the words of one of his colleagues, "couldn't really quite do the work" that Ben's kindness became at times "counter-productive." Some of these people managed to get through the program, but others did not, and to have admitted them, especially if better-qualified students were consequently denied admission, would appear to constitute a disservice to everyone concerned. If Ben was wrong-headed in this matter, however, at least we have further evidence to support the idea that our vices are merely extensions of our virtues.

This tendency of Ben's to "back losers," as one graduate student (who claimed to dislike Ben for that reason) put it, was justified, if in no other way, by a wonderful hoax perpetrated by two of his colleagues on the Woodrow Wilson Fellowship selection committee, Paul Hardacre, Professor of History at Vanderbilt, and Ray Poggenburg, Head of the Department of French at Vanderbilt. The following account was provided by Lyell Behr, who was on the committee but was not in on the joke:

For whatever reason, Ben had a special affinity for the unusual candidate. If candidates had gotten a degree while in jail or had some unusual background, such as having served in the Hungarian army or whatever, Ben would support them. He was not for people who got lots of A's but had never read a book or play other than what they had in their college courses. On one occasion Paul Hardacre dreamed up a candidate who had all the properties he knew Ben would appreciate but who had only indifferent grades. I don't remember much detail, but they even had a photo. Ben supported her very strongly, and then Hardacre and Poggenburg were negative. I didn't know what to think--I was not part of the plan. on the one hand, I wanted to support Ben, but there were those grades. Anyway, Hardacre and Poggenburg finally admitted the hoax; Ben enjoyed the whole thing as much as any of us.

In addition to the grades, according to Richard Marius, who came onto the committee the following year, Hardacre and Poggenburg had forged letters of recommendation praising her as brilliant but implying that she had worked her way through college as a prostitute. When the two argued against her, Marius has written, "Ben objected furiously that they might reject her merely because she had been a prostitute and had worked her way through school with what she had."

Kindness, generosity, and this almost perverse desire to be fair pervaded the atmosphere of his classroom, even in his discussions of authors and their works. He almost always presented a writer in the best possible light; he did not ignore flaws, but he did not dwell on them. He concentrated on facts and what could be said in favor of his subject. The reasons for his emphasis on the positive were many, but two of the most important in regard to his teaching were, first, his desire to pass on to others his own love of literature, which had given him such pleasure, and, second, his distaste for and distrust of second-hand judgments. Pressed for his estimation of John Lydgate in the first half of the British literature survey, he was careful to preface his statement with both an outline of the extensive reading of primary material upon which his opinion was based and an emphatic declaration that it was, after all, his opinion. Only then was he willing to voice his view that Lydgate was very much inferior to Chaucer, afterwards giving a number of specific reasons why he thought so. I can still hear him upbraiding an anonymous student after he had handed back the mid-term test in that course: "Do not say that John Lydgate was a second-rate poet if you have not read a great deal of John Lydgate's poetry." Since, for some reason, students tend to parrot negative more readily than positive judgments and because Ben hated to be parroted, he generally refrained from saying anything of that sort.

Of course, the main reason his comments were usually positive was that he really did enjoy most of the things he taught. Asked late in his life if he would do something else were he given the chance to begin again, he said he would not, and why not? "Well," he said, "I've liked some of the students and most of the books."

Chapter Two

Ben Drew Kimpel, Jr., was born November 6, 1915, to Ben Drew and Gladys Crane Kimpel in Fort Smith, Arkansas. His father died a few weeks before Ben's third birthday. Except for one year in a west coast military academy, he received his elementary education and two years of his secondary education in the Fort Smith public schools. He attended an eastern prep school for two years before entering Harvard University, where he took his A.B. and A.M. degrees, going on to North Carolina for his doctorate. He served in the U.S. Army between August 1942 and March 1946, and was with the State Department from 1946 to 1951, at which time he returned to Harvard for post-doctoral studies in medieval literature before joining the faculty at the University of Arkansas at Fayetteville, where he remained until his death on April 21, 1983.

The bare outline of one life is apt to sound very like that of any other, and, as the foregoing paragraph demonstrates, the life of Ben Kimpel is no exception. Such a summary does little more than block out the canvas and lay down the broad strokes that roughly define the shape, the approximate spatial limits of a portrait. The roughed-in sketch may have a certain harmony of its own, but the character and soul of the subject emerge gradually, stroke by stroke. It is hoped that the following chronological account of Ben's life may fill in a few of the blank spaces and begin to provide definition and clarity to our portrait.

1915-1942

Any account of Ben Kimpel's childhood has to be pieced together from a scattering of documents and the very few facts that he mentioned himself. Except for a year in Los Angeles (1924-1925), he lived in Fort Smith from his birth until he went off to Phillips Exeter Academy in the autumn of 1931.

Ben attended Peabody Elementary School in Fort Smith, where—in the third grade, at least—one would hardly have guessed from his performance what he was to become. He was absent from school all but five of the thirty days in the first six-week period, apparently beginning the semester five weeks late, and missed sixteen and a half of the twenty-eight days in the second. At mid-term he had A's in arithmetic, deportment, and health; B's in reading and language; C's in spelling and music, and D's in drawing and penmanship. At year's end, after having attended eighty-eight and a half of ninety days, he had made an A in geography, which he picked up at mid-term and for which he had received a C at the end of the first grading period, As again in health and deportment; B's in spelling, reading, arithmetic, and language; no C's; he maintained his D's in penmanship and drawing and made an E in music. ("'E' means the pupil is among the poorest in the class and will probably fail unless his school work improves," reads the note printed on the back of the report card.)

Evidently, he was a clean, polite little boy (A's in health and deportment), and he must have worked very hard for that B in spelling; he was the first to admit that he was a C speller at best. I would guess that the beginning of his passion for geography that went along with his great love of traveling can be pretty precisely dated toward the end of February 1924, after which time he made all A's in the subject. And he must have been made to sing for his music grade. Despite being tone-deaf, Ben loved music. He also loved to sing. And he was just awful; he simply could not carry a tune. I think it sounded all right to him; although they can often tell if someone else is off-key, being oblivious to their own cacophony· is a great blessing to the tone-deaf and a curse to all those around them.

Anyone who ever tried to decipher Ben's comments on a paper will have no trouble understanding the D's in penmanship. The earliest sample of his writing that I have dates from 1927; in fifty-six years, his hand did not change at all. He wrote at the age of sixty-seven exactly as he did at eleven.

Despite his mediocre performance at Peabody—or perhaps because of it—it was about this time that his mother engaged a French tutor for the eight-year-old Ben. It is not known for how long the tutor was engaged, but it was long enough for Ben to learn French reasonably well and to reveal both his gift for learning languages and the pleasure he derived from it. In time, Ben's complete mastery of French and, later, German made him, by anyone's standards, trilingual.

In Southern California, where the family moved in the summer of 1924, Ben was enrolled in the Urban Military Academy in Los Angeles and received special recognition in the form of the following citation:

SUPER-HONOR CARD

This is to Certify that Cadet Kimpel has, by his meritorious Conduct, received four Honor Cards in succession. He has been an honor to the academy that he represents, and all the academy staff praises such conduct from its cadets. The commandant feels that he has been a credit to the corps Of cadets, a credit to his parents and a credit to himself. For this reason, he is awarded the Super-Honor cadet card.

George BAILEY, Major, Headmaster
[Signed] Roy W. Park, Major, Commandant

Ben's father was born in the Arkansas delta town of Dermott. Ben often visited his paternal grandparents and other relatives there, and after his father's death in 1918, Ben and his mother continued to maintain their ties with the family. Ben's grandfather used to take his first and, at the time, his only grandson to the local movie theater for the Saturday afternoon matinees. Miss Evelyn Bowden, a former resident of Dermott, has reported that between 1917 and 1920 she and her friends always made a point of not sitting near Mr. Dave Kimpel when they went to the theater because "he read all of the captions out loud to his little grandson." How often Ben visited after 1920 Miss Bowden cannot say since not only did talkies appear but also by then he had undoubtedly learned to read for himself whatever captions there were, and Miss Bowden remembers his existence only because of the annoyance his grandfather created on his account.

That he felt a certain nostalgia for the visits to Southeast Arkansas with its flat land, crawfish, and red-winged blackbirds seems likely; among the slides from a "sentimental journey" that he took in the spring of 1971 is a shot of the Lephieuw cotton gin in Dermott. His grandfather had been a part owner of the gin, which was torn down a year or so after Ben took the photograph. Judging from Ben's own characterization of himself as a child, he was just the sort of child he wouldn't have liked very much. He admitted that he absolutely badgered his mother into sending him off on his first trip to Europe when he was eleven. His plan had succeeded by the summer before his twelfth birthday, for his first passport, issued jointly with his uncle, Davis Crane, is dated June 17, 1927.

[Itinerary in Ben's hand--note misspellings: Ille [Ile], Harve [Le Havre], Ambasador [Ambassador], Avingon [Avignon], Sorento [Sorrento], Lucern [Lucerne or Luzern], Strasburg [Strasbourg], Glascow [Glasgow).]

[Map with route marked with black ink—became the habit of a lifetime.)

On the return trip, although the itinerary does not indicate it, the two made a second stop in New York, staying at least long enough to attend a performance of "Hit the Deck" starring Brian Donlevy at the Belasco Theatre on 44th Street. Since the souvenir playbill was for the week beginning August 29, they must have attended the evening performance on the day they arrived in New York, Sunday, September 4; the Monday performance would have featured a new playbill. This event proved to be one of considerable importance because it was the beginning of one of Ben's greatest pleasures: Broadway musicals, particularly those from the 1930s and '40s. His large record collection included dozens of complete show scores, and he knew the lyrics and, in principle, the tunes of all of them.

After silent movies, a French tutor, a military academy, the Grand Tour, and a Broadway show, the next big influence on Ben seems to have been scouting. Before joining the Boy Scouts of America, he was involved for at least one summer with an Indiana organization known as the Woodcrafters. In the summer of 1929, he attended a Woodcrafter camp on Isle Royale, where between July 24 and August 15, he successfully completed the requirements for becoming a Silver "C" Woodcrafter. He qualified with exactly the required number of points in each of three categories: athletics (7 points), military (4 points), and "Culvercraft" (29 points).

The tests he passed for his forty points as well as the ones he either did not pass or did not attempt provide an interesting profile of Ben at fourteen. Here are the ones he passed:

ATHLETICS:
    Swim 100 yards (Compulsory)--4 pts.
    Dive correctly from the surface and recover articles from the bottom in at least 6 feet of water--1 pt.
    Demonstrate the resuscitation of drowning using the Schaefer method--2 pts.
MILITARY:
    Pass B test in Woodcraft Regulations (Compulsory)--1 pt
    Win two notches in the current year--1 pt.
    Must be proficient in the school of the squad and pass a test in conducting the drill of a squad in a close order (Compulsory)--2 pts.
CULVERCRAFT:
    Send and receive satisfactorily a message with wireless buzzer, and know parts of a simple wireless receiver and transmitting set--3 pts.
    Send and receive satisfactorily a message by semaphore at the rate of at least 30 letters per minute--2 pts.
    Know the elementary rules of camp hygiene and tell how to choose a campsite (Compulsory)--1 pt.
    Demonstrate and have proper knowledge of the use and care of a canoe--1 pt.
    Know how to find directions without the aid of a compass--1 pt.
    Identify and describe twenty birds (Compulsory)--5 pts.
    Identify and give satisfactory descriptions of forty plants and distinguish common poisonous plants and berries (Compulsory)--5 pts.
    Recognize and describe twenty trees (Compulsory)—5 pts.

Name and point out six constellations of stars other than those required for the Bronze "C"--2 pts.

Know five of the common reptiles, describe their life habits and usefulness to man--1 pt.

Tie quickly and tell the use of 15 different knots—2 pts.

Cook "twists" and flapjacks in the open--1 pt.

And then there were the things he did not do.

ATHLETICS:

Have been a member of a divisional baseball, basketball, or volleyball team

High jump, 4 ft. or more

Running broad jump, 13 ft. or more

100 yard dash, 13 sec. or less

25 yard swim, free style, 24 sec. or less

40 yard swim, on back, 52 sec. or less

First in a track meet

Satisfactory graceful, fancy, or high diving

Winner of a scheduled boxing match, 3 rounds or more

Winner of a scheduled tennis match, at least 3 sets

MILITARY:

Have had an "A" discipline grade for 3 weeks

Qualify as Marksman

CULVERCRAFT:

Make one of the articles of handicraft prescribed for the Silver "C"

Demonstrate and have proper knowledge of the use and care of a rowboat

Make a second article of handicraft approved for the Silver "C"

Present a satisfactory diary of five weeks of camp life in the Woodcraft School

Write a satisfactory article or news item for the "Woodcrafter"

Ben was also a Boy Scout and attended camp in Fayetteville. The camp was held on what is now called Markham Hill, and Mrs. Markham is reported to have remarked to a student in the sixties who had mentioned that Dr. Kimpel was his favorite teacher, "Oh, you mean Ben Kimpel! I knew him when he was a little fat boy because he came up here to the Boy Scout Camp one summer."

Regardless of the limitations his girth may have imposed upon him, Ben was a successful scout, achieving the rank of Eagle Scout. In a tribute that appeared soon after his death, Matt Horan mentions this accomplishment and notes that one of his merit badges was in Latin, the test having been administered by a Fort Smith clergyman. But Ben's strength was not exclusively mental; the energy and stamina, not to mention the grace, of his 5'10" frame, which carried anywhere between two hundred and thirty upwards to three hundred pounds throughout his adult life, was also remarkable. As late as 1976, he was climbing ladders to view the kivas at Bandelier, hiking difficult canyon trails for hours in the blazing sun, and clambering in and out of a rubber raft on a Colorado River float trip. The body that can do that sort of thing every day for two weeks out of the year after leading a sedentary existence for most of the other fifty and going through two to four packs of unfiltered Camels daily commands a certain respect at the very least.

A few months before his sixteenth birthday, Ben left Fort Smith for Exeter, New Hampshire, to attend Phillips Exeter Academy, which was and continues to be one of the premier preparatory schools in the country. Edward Thayer, one of Ben's classmates, writes, "Ben and I arrived at Exeter in the fall of '31 somewhat overwhelmed, as any young man would be, on arriving from the hinterlands to such an august institution as Exeter." He remembers Ben as "quiet, shy, [and] very smart" and adds that he had "a good sense of humor."

During his two years of preparation at Exeter, Ben—or Benny, as he was known to his classmates--was a member of the Lantern Club, a literary society the primary activities of which were sponsoring lectures and attending weekly dinners, and was on the contributing staff of the school literary magazine, The Monthly , for which he wrote two poems and three short stories. These five extant examples of juvenilia are compelling evidence of the finality of death, for it is almost certain that, had it been possible, Ben would have returned to this life to prevent their discovery. As the work of a bright sixteen year old, they are not bad, but neither do they indicate that any great talent either as a poet or as a writer of fiction lay waiting to be stirred. The themes are interesting insofar as they reflect Ben's mind at the time.

"War Slogans" (January, 1932), an anti-war poem in the vein of the World War I poets Sasseen and Owen, addresses, like Owen's "Dulce et Decorum Est," the discrepancy between the rhetoric of war and its grim realities, an idea with which Ben was concerned all of his life. He maintained, in the late 1970s, that World War II, the war, incidentally, that he served in, was the last war that the United States had been involved in that was fought "for a clear purpose." The possibility that any war is necessary or just is implicitly denied in "War Slogans," and Ben certainly modified that position, but quite aside from the question of whether wars were just or unjust, he always thought that warfare ought not be glorified, but seen for what it was.

"Cynicism" (April, 1932) asks and answers four questions. The responses to the first three--What is Life? What is Wealth? What is Honor?--are very cynical. The poem concludes, "What are Cynics?/They tell us things we do not need and do not want to know." Ben struggled, not always successfully, against a tendency toward cynicism himself; in fact, this struggle may well have been responsible for strengthening the characteristics that ultimately dominated his world-view, benevolence and generosity. one of his short stories, "Tom, Dick, and Mary" (November, 1932), is a rather clever but undeniably cynical tale of a teen-age love triangle. The story is successful in at least one respect: the characters are not meant to be appealing, and indeed they are not; both Dick and Mary are disloyal, self-serving, hypocritical, opportunistic, and cruel, and it is difficult to feel much sympathy for Tom, who is childish, insecure, naive, and gullible.

Most people would never associate the bleak view of human relationships offered in this story with the Ben Kimpel they knew, but it was there even in his maturity and informed more than a few of his attitudes. The generosity of his estimation of other people was by no means naive; he was quite aware of the existence of vices great and small in others and in himself, but he did what he could to eliminate his own or at least render them as ineffective as possible, and he had a gift for interacting with other people in such a way as to avoid or diminish the force of their vices. It was hard to find an opening for pettiness, cruelty, malice, or viciousness in a conversation with Ben.

The central character in another of the short stories, "A Modern Melodrama" (March 1933], is also an innocent victimized by insensitive and cruel people. This character, Lew, elicits a little more sympathy than the guileless Tom of "Tom, Dick, and Mary," but he still lacks the depth or complexity necessary for the reader to be much affected by his fate. The story is interesting for two reasons: first, Ben tried his hand at writing in dialect--with no great success; second, it might pique the interest of a psychologist because, as in "Tom, Dick, and Mary," a woman, selfish and, in this case, openly vicious, abuses the central character. Her partner in making Lew miserable is her father. In both stories, then, a man and a woman conspire to exclude the main character from some sort of intimate circle, yet they wish to keep him near at hand so that they may use him and vent their cruelty on him.

The third story, "Henry" (May, 1932], is a rather strained and uneven attempt to portray a rich boy's discomfort with his debt of gratitude to his mother's gardener, who had saved his life during the war. The following exchange is from the flashback to the battlefield on which the rich boy was injured and should be enough to make us grateful that Ben finally preferred reading short stories to writing them.

"Do you think you can crawl along if I help you? Our trenches are over there."

"Yes. My leg feels better." Even as he said it, he felt a pain so sharp that he could not keep back an "Oh."

After these youthful attempts, Ben's only other known venture into fiction writing was a novel; I don't know when he wrote it--it could have been any time between the late '30s and early '60s. The only things I do know about it are that Duncan Eaves had read it and pronounced it laughably bad, that the word 'Baptist' turned up in it often--always spelled 'Babtist,' and that Ben destroyed it. Duncan took enormous delight in telling people about Ben's novel and in needling him with "Spell Baptist for us, Ben--come on, Ben, spell Baptist for us!" No wonder Ben burned the thing--not that destroying it stopped Duncan from tormenting him with it.

Ben's academic performance at Exeter was not outstanding, although he brought his average up enough to be in the Cum Laude Society by the time he graduated. For most of his career there, however, he was listed in the Second Honors group, that is, among the students whose grade average was "nearer a B than a C." One grading period he made a D in an English literature course, and when, many months after Ben's death, his sister showed the report card to Duncan, Duncan betrayed the same puckish glee that Ben's misspelling of Baptist had occasioned.

After graduating from Exeter in 1933, although he had listed Northwestern as his college preference in the Exeter yearbook, the Pean, Ben went directly to Harvard, taking his A.B. with Honors in 1937. On June 21, 1937, he was notified of his election to Phi Beta Kappa. The letter and the certificate, which he received the following Friday, June 25, were signed by the Secretary-Treasurer of the organization, Arthur M. Schlesinger, Jr., who had also been in Ben's graduating class at Phillips Exeter.

Although as an undergraduate he chose English as his field of concentration, Ben's plans as late as 1937 were to pursue a career in law, and he enrolled in Harvard Law School for one term, long enough to discover that was not what he wanted at all. He returned to the study of letters and in 1939 received his A.M. The same year that he earned his Masters at Harvard, he went to the University of North Carolina, Chapel Hill, to begin work toward his Ph.D. in literature, his major field being American literature with a minor in medieval. It was in 1939 that he met T. C. Duncan Eaves, who had been at Chapel Hill as an undergraduate and had gone on to Harvard for his doctorate, having taken an M.A. at the University of Cincinnati. Eaves returned to Chapel Hill often for week-end parties with the friends he had made there as an undergraduate, and it was on one of these occasions that he and Ben were introduced by mutual friends. According to Eaves, the week-end was an especially wild one, and the two young men spent most of it in each other's company. The relationship developed quickly and, except for that with his mother, would prove to be the most important of Ben's life.

From September 1940 until May 1942, Ben had a teaching fellowship at Chapel Hill which entailed teaching one course each term in freshman English for $55 a month. He received his Ph.D. in the spring of 1942; his thesis was entitled "Herman Melville's Thought After 1851." He returned to Fort Smith following graduation, and on August 7, 1942, enlisted in the Army.

<h2 style="text-align:center">1942-1946</h2>

Ben's first assignment in the Army was to the reception center at Camp Robinson, Arkansas, where he served in the classification section for eleven months.

At Camp Robinson, Ben and a number of his co-workers began going out to eat once a week, usually Friday or Saturday evening. Their preferred restaurant was the Canton Tea Garden on Main Street in Little Rock, which, besides serving very good Chinese food, featured booths with curtains that could be pulled together for privacy, and in one of these the little group of five or six would sit for hours, eating, talking, and playing Botticelli. The group included Ray Brock, Leonard Peters, Powell Compere, Rayburn Moore, and Dolphus and Marie Whitten; all of the members were single except, of course, the Whittens.

Mr. Brock worked with Ben every day in classification between August 1942 and April 1943, at which time Mr. Brock went to Florida for his officer training. "Ben ranked very high in my estimation," Mr. Brock said. "His character, his work, everything about him was simply tops, and," he added rather puckishly, "he didn't mind a bit being fat."

Mr. Whitten also remembered Ben from those months at Camp Robinson:

> I must tell you about Ben as a military person. Anyone who knows Ben would know that neither physically nor mentally nor emotionally was he the military type, in the sense that not only did he not believe in war, but he also didn't believe in inconvenience. And he wasn't alone, you understand, in that regard.
>
> The first impression I had of Ben was that his uniform didn't fit; the pants hit him at the ankle, and they were always too tight around the waist because of the way he was built, and so he wouldn't have passed as one of the sharpest soldiers.

We used to call him The Gnome because he had a rather fat tummy, he was sort of pear-shaped—or—I'm not sure how to describe it--but his uniform struck him somewhere on the ankles, and he was not a large person then, but he was weighted at the middle, shall we say, and he really looked like a little gnome.

Ben was a calm and even-tempered person. He didn't have much patience with bureaucracy or the Army way of doing things, but he didn't make an issue of it. He adjusted himself to the situation.

The general impression was that here was a very bright man, a very gentle, quiet person, one with a lot of wit and a playful kind of intellect, who was delightful to be around. He had such a good sense of humor. Just a charming man—very unassuming, and so polite. He never made a point of his brilliance; you just knew that he was bright; he never called attention to himself.

Ben's duties in classification largely consisted of interviewing draftees who came first to Camp Robinson to be processed before being sent out to various parts of the country for training. According to Mr. Whitten, most of the people in 'classification had college degrees, and many were school administrators or teachers in civilian life. To give an idea of the sorts of encounters Ben was likely to have had in his job, Mr. Whitten related the following incident which occurred soon after he had been moved to classification from the assignment section:

A man came in. I asked him his name; he talked with—I didn't know if it was New England or Brooklyn or what—
some kind of accent that was strange to me. And I said, "What is your permanent address?"

"Erster Bay."

Well, I'd just never heard anyone say "erster" for "oyster," so I had to get him to spell it.

"Jeez! *Erster*—o-y-s-t-e-r. Erster Bay, Lung Goiland!"

"And what is your work specialty?"

"I'm a flanger."

I said, "I'm sorry, but you're from a different part of the country, and this is probably a different occupation from what I'd be familiar with; what do you do?"

"I flang."

"And what do you—flang?"

"Well--the rivets on a bulkhead."

"You flang rivets on the bulkhead; you're in shipbuilding?"

"Sure!"

Another story Ben told about himself concerns his arrival at Camp Robinson. It seems another recruit struck up a conversation with Ben and asked where he was from. "I come from Fort Smith," Ben said. "I *came* from Fort Smith," the recruit solicitously corrected him. Ben was largely free of the pride of learning, but this must have irked him a little.

Mr. Whitten has reported that, despite having to deal with such characters as these, Ben was quite serious about his work in classification, and "of course, he did his job very well."

Since both Whitten and Brock left Camp Robinson before Ben, neither knew when Ben left or where he went, and Ben's military records give no details of his service in the states except to state that "he spent five months as a Classification Specialist and six months interviewing personnel." It is also noted in his record that he attended a twelve-week intensive French course at the University of North Carolina at Chapel Hill, and although no dates are given, he probably took this course just prior to his departure for Europe in March of 1944 as a chief clerk and interpreter for the French Civil Affairs Detachment.

The exact date of Ben's departure from Camp Robinson is not known, but his destination was Camp McCain, south of Grenada, Mississippi. Although no official evidence that he was stationed at Camp McCain for most of 1943 has been found, unofficial evidence strongly suggests that this was the case. In the autumn of 1981, Ben recorded the major places he had visited each year from 1922 through the summer of 1981. The list is on spiral notebook paper and written in pencil. The entry for 1942 is "Little Rock" and that for 1943 is simply "Mississippi." On a map, one of hundreds that he collected over his sixty years of traveling, he traced the routes he took on various trips between 1938 and 1944 in Arkansas, Louisiana, and Mississippi, and he penned in at their appropriate locations both Camp Robinson and Camp McCain.

Ben left for England on March 23, 1944, arriving April 3. He embarked for Normandy on June 19, 1944, but inclement weather prevented a landing until June 29. During those ten days on the English Channel one thing he did to pass the time was read *Das Kapital*.

Once on the continent, he spent the next nine months in Normandy and Northern France. He must have met, very soon after his arrival in France, a young poet named Paul M. Fontaine; for among Ben's books was a volume of Mr. Fontaine's poetry, *Jeunesse du ciel*, published in 1940, that was presented to Ben in September 1944. The inscription reads in part "A mon ami Ben Kimpel 'Vice-Roi de la Poésie' et 'Prince de Traducteurs.' En souvenir de nos entretiens lyriques et de nos soirées gastronomiques." Fontaine lived some twenty kilometers from the Belgian border in Vervins, where, to judge from the routes radiating from that point that Ben marked on the map of France dated 1944-45, Ben must have spent a considerable length of time before he continued into Belgium in March and Holland in early April of 1945.

On April 12, 1945, he received his commission as 2nd Lieutenant and returned to Romilly, France, for a twelve-day orientation course before going into occupied Germany as a Public Education Officer on April 27, 1945. There, according to his service records, he "directed and supervised the administration and curriculum of Institutions of Learning, including University of Erlangen, 4 High Schools and 16 Grade Schools in the American Occupation Zone of Germany. Also supervised subordinate personnel in the educational department of the governmental units. Screened 1500 School employees and discharged Nazi personnel or persons who were connected with the Nazi party."

One of the few "war stories" I heard Ben tell concerned the opening of the University of Erlangen. His superior officer arrived in Erlangen some days after Ben and said, "Now, the first thing we have to do is get this university back in operation," to which Ben responded, "I've already done that." He said it never occurred to him that he needed orders from higher up to do what obviously had to be done.

Since his job as Public Education Officer spanned only seven and a half months, Ben interviewed an average of two hundred people a month or about forty-five a week between the end of April and mid-December 1945. The interviews, of course, were conducted in German.

For two weeks after his tour of duty as education officer was over and before he was released from active duty, he served as a Battery Motor Officer--that is, a maintenance officer.

I'm not sure whether the brevity of the assignment is an indication of its having been simply an interim job given him to mark time until his discharge or a reflection of his aptitude for it. In any case, he left Europe toward the end of January 1946 and received his discharge at Jefferson Barracks, Missouri, on March 2, 1946. He had been in the service for forty-three months, the last ten as a commissioned officer. He left the Army as a 2nd Lieutenant.

1946-1952

Following his discharge, Ben returned to his home in Fort Smith. In June, he and his mother traveled to Richardson Grove, California, to visit her daughter, Mrs. Charles E.

Warner, who was there with her son, Bill, for the summer. From Richardson Grove, Ben and his mother toured the Pacific Northwest, driving up the coasts of California, Oregon, and Washington and going as far north as Vancouver. Upon their return to Richardson Grove in late July, Ben received word that he had been accepted for diplomatic service by the State Department and was to report in Washington, D.C., on the first of August for six weeks' training in the foreign service school.

On Wednesday, July 24, Ben flew back to Fort Smith, accompanied by his mother, and left the following Monday for Washington. He completed his special training on or about September 11, 1946, and was appointed to the American embassy in Vienna. He flew to Fort Smith on September 14 for a five-day visit with his mother and other relatives before flying to New York. He sailed from New York September 26 on the Marine Marlin for Le Havre, where he apparently took a train to Vienna. At a checkpoint on the German border, he encountered Ray Brock, who was inspecting passports. They had not seen each other since they had been together at Camp Robinson--and, although for some thirty years they lived less than three hundred miles apart, they never saw each other again.

Ben sent a brief entry to the Harvard Class of 1937 Decennial Report (Cambridge, 1947): "Vice-Consul, U.S. Legation, Vienna, Austria. A.M. Harvard 1939. Ph.D. North Carolina. Taught English two years." The following account of some aspects of Ben's life in Vienna comes from Brynhild Rowberg, who retired in 1973, ending a career of more than twenty-five years with the Foreign Service:

> If I remember correctly, Ben arrived in Vienna about 1947 and was immediately assigned to live--in occupied Vienna there was then no choice as to where one might live--in a large house on the Strudlhofgasse, at the top of the Liechtenstein Stiege. He shared his quarters with two colleagues, Andy Olson and Mike Gannett. The address couldn't be more "echt Wienerisch."
>
> Later on he was able to rent a large and elegant apartment on (I think) the Michaelerplatz, quarters which were splendid for entertaining even if they were gloomy and cold. There wasn't much heat in Vienna in those days. In fact, the atmosphere of the city at that time is best depicted in the movie "The Third Man," and I seem to recall that Ben was one of the group that witnessed the filming of a notable scene in the picture, Joseph Cotton pursuing Orson Welles across Wien am Hof and into the entrance to the sewers.
>
> At the office Ben quickly proved himself to be gifted at political analysis, after having served for a short period in the visa section. He also took care of protocol duties at the Legation, a very minor and quickly done part of his job in

the political section. I can't remember how the work was divided in the section, but do know that for a considerable length of time he did political reporting, i.e., analysis of the internal situation in Austria, analysis of the politics and actions of the other occupying powers insofar as they affected Austria's politics and the international situation. He could draft (State Departmentese for "write") quickly and lucidly, and after his departure the then Charge d'Affaires, Walter Dowling, remarked ruefully that Ben was sadly missed.

I don't think that Ben was an especially gifted linguist, but he made up in diligence for any lack of a natural "ear" for languages. His German was good, and I seem to remember that throughout his stay in Vienna he worked on his Russian. There was, unfortunately, not much chance to use this language despite the presence in the city of thousands of Russians. The latter were all too well aware of the dangers inherent in even casual contact with foreigners of any kind. He did, however, have an occasional opportunity to speak Russian at official functions but of course conversation had to be confined to the smallest of small talk. No Russian could venture to engage in a substantive conversation.

Ben was considered the intellectual star of the group assigned to Vienna at that period. He was, however, modest and unpretentious at all times.

Although, as Ms. Rowberg suggests and as students of history or readers of spy novels know, post-war Vienna was a very interesting place to be from a political point of view, whenever Ben spoke of those years, he was usually commenting on Vienna's cultural life, which apparently continued despite either the destruction visited upon the city during the war or the international intrigue of the post-war years and of which Ben took full advantage. It was also there that Ben learned to dance the Viennese waltz with its grand, sweeping movements and dizzying tempo.

Perry Dillon, who began his graduate studies in Fayetteville in the late fifties, once commented to Ben that, when he had visited Vienna, he had found it rather disappointing. Ben's response, according to Mr. Dillon, "was something like: 'Ah, how can you not love Vienna? There's nothing like dancing under the stars all night in Vienna!'" Because Ben rarely spoke of his past and because most people would have felt it an impertinence to ask him about it, such glimpses into his personal life, by virtue of their being surrounded by mystery, excited and fascinated his devotees. I asked Ms. Rowberg if she knew anything about Ben's having danced all night under the stars, and here is her reply:

Toward the end of my own tour of duty in Vienna, and certainly throughout much of the time Ben was stationed there, it was possible to dance all night--

rarely under the stars--in the city. In the late '40s the Viennese revived the custom of Fasching, pre-Lenten balls, and Ben was as delighted as the rest of us to take part in some of these events. Guests at the balls were primarily Austrians, but foreigners resident in the city were often included. I have an idea that Ben was one of a party which attended a·New Year's Eve ball where the symbols of good luck for the New Year were presented: artificial mushrooms (red and white) and a live piglet. Probably a chimney sweep in full regalia, too.

Ben took a course in protocol as part of his training, and overseeing preparations for dinner parties at the Legation, which included, of course, the appropriate seating of the guests, was, as Ms. Rowberg pointed out, one of his minor responsibilities. Juliet Eaves told us that for years after Ben came to Fayetteville, Duncan, who knew very well how to seat guests at dinner, would say to Ben, in wry deference to Ben's former official capacities, "You do that, Ben." And Ben would obligingly rattle off the proper arrangement: "So-and-so sits here; so-and-so sits here; so-and-so sits here . . ." and so on.

A fine impression of another part of his life in Vienna comes from Dr. Valentine Hegstrom in the following letter:

Dear Ms. Wink!

Thank you very much for your letter March 21-86. I will be very happy to help you about Mr. Ben Kimpel's life in Vienna since this had changed my life also. My mother Lydia Hogstrom-Winogradoff happened to be a very talented language teacher (she was a graduate of law school in St. Petersburg - Russia before the revolution--so called Women's college of Bestonshev and she also graduated from University of Belgrade Yugoslavia--French and Russian literature). When Americans came to Vienna, she became a very successful Russian teacher in Berlitz school.

Mr. Ben Kimpel who came with the state department as first secretary of American Embassy in Vienna started to study Russian since he was attending different meetings with Russians in Vienna since the city was occupied by all Allied powers. He was studying very intensely--my mother was giving him many private lessons and soon he was speaking fluently Russian and was studying Russian literature and history and enjoyed reading Tolstoy and Dostoevsky in originals.

At that time my mother did not know where I was since I was taken by Soviet authorities just before the end of the war, May 2, 1945, out of the Swedish consulate where I was employed and since that time she did not know where I was. Soviet authorities have denied any knowledge about my whereabouts. Finally, when I was able to send messages out of Russia in 1946 when Austrian war prisoners were sent home and carne to my mother and told her that I was kept as civilian prisoner in Odessa, my mother with help of her American friends through American Red Cross had sent a message to Finland (I was Finnish citizen). Finnish government asked for my release. My mother, of course, was always worrying and concerned about me because I was her only son, but she was happy that I was alive. American diplomats who preceded Mr. Ben Kimpel started the steps for my release since I was Finnish citizen--Washington authorities have notified Finnish government. When Ben found out from my mother about all these problems he told her--if your 22n will ever return--since he had so many problems with the Russians he should come to the United States with you and he offered to be my sponsor to immigrate into the U.S. and followed through with this.

I was released in July 1947 to Finland and in spring 1948 I came to Vienna since I was to continue my medical school at University of Vienna and stay with my mother. I met Mr. Ben Kimpel in March 1948--he was coming to my mother for Russian language lessons 2-3 times weekly and met with other pupils for conversation. My mother was very fond of him as a student because he had a wonderful memory and he spoke Russian surprisingly well in a short time and knew Russian literature. He had an important job at the embassy but he was always very polite and modest. He also spoke perfect German and soon he knew Viennese dialect and all local cultural life and music and opera.

My mother and I respected him a lot and because he was my sponsor I have obtained my immigration visa just in time when I finished my medical school in 1951 and we went by boat to New York in 1952. Ben Kimpel was already home in Arkansas. Unfortunately my mother became ill with cancer prior to our departure and we had great difficulties but Ben helped us also financially in the beginning until I started my internship and was able to repay him.

Later on when my son Larry was born he accepted to become his godfather.

When I met him in Vienna he was always very relaxed, he smoked his Camel cigarettes, and was very thoughtful. I have never known Americans before but all Austrian pupils in my mother's school had respected and loved him.

I do not have any pictures from that time, but I know my mother frequently for holidays or other occasions was giving him Russian books--mostly classics-- Pushkin, Tolstoy, Lermontov, Dostoyevski in Russian and Ben was reading those books in original. When I visited him in Fayetteville he showed me the books my mother had given him with her inscriptions in Russian.

Lydia Hegstrom and her son, Valentine, settled in Chicago, where he established his medical practice and has continued to practice for over thirty years. Mrs. Hegstrom died in 1956, "before she could visit Ben's home," Dr. Hegstrom wrote, "but at least she had seen me established. I believe Ben visited her before her passing."

"Ben was a great man," Dr. Hegstrom continued, "so very fine, cultured and he knew a lot, so many languages and literatures . . . . My mother was so thankful to Ben and always admired him as a brilliant mind and appreciated his kindness to us and other people."

As far as I know, no one, neither his friends nor members of his family, knew the whole story of Ben's involvement with the Hogstroms. It came to light only after Ben's death, when Dr. Hegstrom's address was found in one of Ben's address books. Duncan and Juliet -Eaves and Ben's sister, Betty Warner, shared the sad task of notifying Ben's distant friends of his death, and Dr. Hegstrom wrote to Mrs. Warner after having received her letter. How many others like the Hogstroms Ben helped we may never know, but as a testament both to his generosity and to his modesty, the story of Valentine and Lydia Hegstrom provides a splendid insight into his humanity.

Duncan Eaves suggested that, had the State Department left Ben in Vienna, he might have made his career in the diplomatic corps. Fortunately for most of us, he was sent back to the states in 1951, and he found his duties in Washington, whatever they may have been, not altogether to his liking.

In the summer of 1951, he returned to Northwest Arkansas to see his mother and other relatives in Fort Smith as well as his good friend Duncan Eaves, who had joined the faculty at the University of Arkansas in Fayetteville some two years earlier. When he visited Duncan in Fayetteville, he was told that there would be a position available the following year, and Duncan suggested that, in the interim, Ben return to Harvard for postdoctoral work in medieval literature. He and Duncan spoke with the other current medievalist at the University, Mary Celeste Parler, to determine whether she had any objections to Ben's coming in with credentials in her field. She assured them that she had none. Ben resigned his position with the State Department and returned to Harvard as a full-time student for the 1951-52 academic year.

On March 30, 1952, some two months before Ben finished his year of post-doctoral work at Harvard, he received a phone call from his brother-in-law, Charles Warner. Ben's mother, Gladys Crane Kimpel Porter, had been killed in an automobile accident.

Ben felt close ties to his family, especially, of course, to his mother and her family. His decision to accept a position at the University in Fayetteville was strongly influenced by the promise of his being so near Fort Smith. The tragedy of his mother's death affected him deeply, and it must have been all the more tragic for him, occurring as it did only a few months before he would return to reside permanently in Northwest Arkansas after a twenty-year absence.

Nonetheless, he went ahead with his plans and arrived in Fayetteville in the autumn of 1952. Aside from the proximity to his relatives in Fort Smith and the presence of his great friend Duncan Eaves and his lovely wife, Juliet, the congeniality of other members of the department as well as the generally amiable atmosphere at the University in those years contributed to Ben's decision to make Fayetteville his home for the rest of his life.

CHAPTER THREE

Ben arrived in Fayetteville in the summer of 1952. He was thirty-six. While he was having his home built across from the Confederate cemetery on Rock Street, he rented a modest but comfortable house on the corner of Jackson Street and Mission Drive, near where Duncan and Juliet Eaves would eventually have their home. That first autumn, he got some idea of the shape his future in Fayetteville was going to take. Duncan Eaves knew Ben well; he knew, for example, just how far he could go with a joke with Ben: a long way, as it happened.

The first official gathering at the university each year was the President's reception, at the time a formal affair to which the women wore long dresses and men were attired in either dinner jackets or tails, and, although Ben always looked very elegant when he dressed up, he never much liked to have to do it. Juliet Eaves has given the following account of the first President's reception that Ben attended:

> Ben had some tails, and they managed to get him into them—and he was very uncomfortable, but they got him into the tails, and Duncan said that by the time they got to the end of the receiving line, Ben was being introduced as 'Mr. Jumbo.' And it made Ben so mad! He said, "I'll never go there again! Make me get dressed up, introduce me as Mr. Jumbo, and then they gave me a glass of Kool-Aid and Oreo cookies!"

The last blow was, to be sure, the hardest for Ben to take. After five years with the u.s. legation in Vienna, he was accustomed to having to dress, and he was not cursed with an ego that would have taken umbrage at the humorous allusion to his girth, but he would have thought it too much to ask of any civilized man to endure them both without good food and drink.

Although he would always be a frequent guest in the Eaves home, during the early years of his life in Fayetteville he was virtually a member of their family. During the autumn of 1952, Juliet was in South Carolina, where she had given birth to their second child in August, and Ben and Duncan were constant companions during her absence. The bond of friendship, first formed in 1939 and maintained primarily from a distance since Ben had left

Chapel Hill in 1942, quickly grew to such strength as to prove indissoluble for the rest of their lives. The relationship between these two immensely witty, intelligent, and learned men delighted and fascinated those around them for over forty years.

Ben Kimpel and T. C. Duncan Eaves appeared to be worlds apart in many ways. In the first place, there was the matter of their physical appearances: Duncan was perhaps six inches shorter than Ben, but he seemed much shorter because he was also small boned and slender. His dapper frame, so erect that one almost had the impression that he leaned ever so slightly backward, was capped by a handsome head of dark hair, and his large, lively, wonderfully expressive eyes looked even larger than they were, magnified by uncommonly thick glasses. His movements were quick and precise, and his every gesture suggested at once both aristocratic elegance and cocky flamboyance, fused, as it were, with an electricity of nervous energy. What has already been said of 'Mr. Jumbo's' appearance should suffice to illustrate the dramatic physical contrast between the two.

Temperamentally, too, they differed, so much so that some of their acquaintances were at pains to understand not simply how they could have been such close friends for so long a time, but how they ever became friends at all. One theory had it that, in a rather sophisticated version of the attraction of opposites, Ben represented the "Apollonian" and Duncan the "Dionysian" aspects of the relationship. In fact, there was a great deal more of the Dionysian in Ben than many people realized; the two had, after all, met during a non-stop party week-end in Chapel Hill back in 1939. Juliet Eaves has described Duncan and his friends as "really wild, party-going people" with whom Ben "fit right in." One week-end when Duncan had come down to Chapel Hill, the group had another of their revels, and Ben's apartment was the scene of the most of their carousing. When it was finally over, Ben and Duncan were left with a colossal mess; Ben took one look at it and, walking out, said, "I'm never coming back here!"

But he did love to party, and many an evening when he and his friends and colleagues in Fayetteville were gathered together for one reason or another, along about ten or eleven o'clock someone would suggest that they go to Ben's house, and off they would go. One of these revellers has recalled that Ben never demurred from this, sometimes even suggesting it himself, and has described what usually happened once they all got to Ben's:

> There was a lot of dancing. He had a big, shaggy throw rug on the lower floor
> of that big room, so that would be got out of the way, the furniture would be got
> out of the way, and that would be converted into a dance floor. Ben liked to
> dance, and he danced very well, but he danced with large gestures. Frequently, it
> was like a scene in the middle of the third reel of those Ginger Rogers-Fred
> Astaire movies: after a while Ben and somebody or other would be dancing--very
> well and with .great gusto and great enthusiasm and wide sweeping arm gestures-

-and no one else would be dancing, or they would be dancing pretty small in the corners.

Ben's record collection, which was enormous, included a great deal of classical music--operas, symphonies, quartets, everything--but he also had a large number of recordings of the Big Bands and other popular music from the thirties and forties, almost all of them the hard shellac 78s, which provided the music for these often spontaneous parties. Ben not only was a very good dancer, extremely quick and light on his feet, but also knew all of the popular dances from the twenties, thirties, and forties; he could do the Charleston, for example, very well, and often did. He was also very adept at jitterbugging, although once he carne very near disaster jitterbugging in a London nightclub. He did not like to go to nightclubs, but one evening when he was in London with Duncan and Juliet Eaves, some friends of theirs took them out to a club where Peggy Lee was going to perform. The dance floor was a very small raised platform around which tables were arranged, and at one of these tables some Duke or other who was a great admirer of Peggy Lee was seated with her. Ben and Juliet were dancing a rather energetic jitterbug when suddenly Ben's feet slipped out from under him and he very nearly fell over onto the Duke's table. Duncan, taking his usual puckish delight in Ben's embarrassment, exclaimed, "Oh, I wish he had fallen into his grapefruit!"

Nobody could bedevil Ben quite the way Duncan could. One of the most striking contrasts between the two was Duncan's fascination with and Ben's total lack of interest in the details of other people's lives. Typical of the situations that grew out of this contrast is one concerning two middle-aged women of their acquaintance. The two women were very good friends, and Duncan thought one of them was much more attractive than the other. The curious thing that interested Duncan so much was that the one he considered the more comely of the two would attract men, and then the men would marry the other. Someone who witnessed all of this has described Duncan and Ben in an exchange that may be taken as emblematic of their differences:

> Duncan was greatly bemused by that, and he'd ask how that could be; this other one was cuter in every way. He just couldn't account for it. Ben wasn't at all interested, but Duncan kept talking to Ben about it--pressing him. Ben would say, "I don't know. I don't know, Duncan. I don't know anything about that."
>
> "But, Ben, you do know!" Duncan would say. "If somebody put a gun to your head--now, Ben, if somebody put a gun to your head and said 'Choose'--you'd choose that little one, wouldn't you?"

Ben said, "No, I'd say shoot!"

That the two were conscious of certain differences in their social attitudes is shown in. a letter from Ben to Duncan, written from England in the autumn of 1960 when Ben was doing research. Ben had spent a week in Paris, and a mutual friend, a woman, had joined him there for the last two days of his stay. Having informed Duncan of this in his letter, he wrote, "please (you like catty remarks) teach your children that even women should have some conversation beyond what the nice people do & how much things cost."

Duncan, always a great talker, also loved to talk on the telephone; Ben, on the other hand, considered the telephone one of the necessary evils of the twentieth century. He had a phone-an old-fashioned black one with a dial--which he used only when it was absolutely necessary. Duncan would sometimes call Ben just to chat, and Ben would say, "I don't have time to talk now. Goodbye" and just hang up. Such brusqueness never made Duncan angry, for he knew that he was perhaps the only person in the world that Ben loved enough and whose love Ben trusted enough to respond to him in such a way. Duncan took pride in the fact, for example, that he was the only person at the University that Ben would tell to get out of his office.

Ben and Duncan enjoyed doing all kinds of things together in addition to partying. For one, they loved to play cards. During Ben's early years in Fayetteville, they played Piquet—virtually every night, according to Duncan, who was apparently a little better or a little luckier at the game than was Ben. Juliet related that "they loved to play Piquet, except Ben would get so mad because Duncan would always win. I'd hear them when they'd play, and Ben would say, 'I'm never going to play with you again!' and throw the cards on the table." But, of course, he kept coming back for more. They were also excellent bridge players. They usually played as partners, and people liked to challenge them. As Juliet has said, "I think [the people who challenged them] were very foolish to take them on; they were both very good. They had the sorts of minds that the minute you bid, they knew exactly what was in everybody's hand." Sometimes Juliet would play with them as Duncan's partner. "Ben used to be very kind," she recalled; "Duncan would jump all over me, and a lot of times Ben would say, 'Now, Duncan, it's your fault you didn't make it--you overbid, so don't blame her.'"

Ben was also very good at poker, so good, in fact, that his being much sought-after for poker games in Fayetteville is evidence of how much people enjoyed his company; they certainly were not very likely to win money from him. In addition to his card sense, Ben had the temperament for poker, patient and unflappable. And, again, that he was anything but unflappable when he played Piquet with Duncan provides another bit of evidence of their quite special relationship.

Oddly enough, it was the frequency of their card-playing that led Ben and Duncan to quite another activity. After some time, Duncan suggested that as long as they were going to be together almost every evening, they may as well do, as Duncan put it, "something constructive." Thus began their scholarly collaboration. Ben's only publication before he went to Fayetteville had been a brief article on Melville which appeared in American Literature in 1944; then in 1953, his "The Narrator of the Canterbury Tales" was published in the prestigious ELH, and a year later Poetry published "John Gould Fletcher in Retrospect." Aside from three papers presented at conferences in 1969, 1971, and 1976, and two other articles which appeared in 1975, the four books and forty-nine articles that represent his published scholarship were all done in collaboration with Eaves.

When Ben arrived in Fayetteville, Duncan was in the midst of editing The Letters of William Gilmore Simms, and Ben both advised him and helped him proofread aloud the five volumes and the index of that work. Duncan wrote in the memorial to Ben published in Paideuma that "such kindness and generosity were typical of him--he always helped students and fellow scholars by sharing with them his knowledge and giving them excellent, rational advice." While Duncan continued his work with Simms' letters, he and Ben began corning up with other plans for working together.

Their first project did not require their considerable talents as researchers: they edited an anthology, The Informal Reader , published by Appleton-Century-Crofts in 1955. The collection of essays, short stories, a play, and poems, most of which are followed by brief comments and a few questions by the editors, was designed for use in freshman composition courses. The introduction reflects several of Ben's ideas about teaching composition and about the relationship between reading and writing which he stuck to for thirty years. Although Ben and Duncan always worked closely together and shared the tasks of research and writing in all of their joint publications, the weight of responsibilities was usually apportioned so that, whereas on one project Ben would :be more or less in charge of doing the   research and Duncan the writing, on another the roles might be reversed. There is no way of proving beyond any question that a sentence, a paragraph, or an entire passage was written by the one or the other, partly because their ideas were generally in harmony and partly because their close association must have resulted in a good deal of mutual influence on style, but in the preface to the anthology some phrases sound so much like Ben when he talked and express so precisely his oft-repeated attitudes toward students and the relationship between reading and writing that they are almost certainly from his hand, although probably smoothed over by his collaborator. The following excerpts contain a number of examples of diction, syntax, and rhetoric typical of

Ben's style, which Duncan referred to, rather disparagingly, as "staccato"; I have underlined phrases that are also typical of Ben's speech.

> . . . above all he [the student) can acquire a feeling for language--not necessarily "fine writing" but for use of words and phrases *which will say exactly what he wants to say*. . . . Our first criterion has been to pick only passages which we like, that is, which we think are successful *in what they try to do and which try to do something worth doing*.
>
> At the same time we have tried to pick only passages which the students may enjoy, or at least read without boredom. We do not believe that it is possible to teach a class which is asleep. . we have not written for an imaginary average, but have tried to keep in mind the brightest members of the class and at the same time *all but the very dullest*.
>
> . . . We have chosen some essays with the idea of stimulating the student to think, of introducing him to new ideas, and of broadening his interests; this purpose is *not unconnected with* the teaching of writing, since a paucity of ideas often limits expression—*it is impossible to write effectively about nothing*, or about topics in which the writer's interest is at most tepid.

The Informal Reader includes a dozen works translated from French, German, or Russian, and, to quote the Preface, "except for the selections from Stefan Zweig and Erich Maria Remarque, the translations are . . . our own." Given Ben's skill in foreign languages and Duncan's sense of style, they thought for a time of making their mark in scholarship as translators. Their next project, a translation published in 1956 of Goethe's *Torquato Tasso*, was to have been, according to a note at the end of the edition, "the first in a series of University of Arkansas editions of standard works not presently available." Their method was based upon their respective strengths; Ben did the direct translation from the verse play, and Duncan was largely responsible for transforming Ben's rough draft into very readable and often elegant blank verse. It is likely that Duncan also had much to do with the final form of Ben's translations for the anthology as well.

The ambition of the projected series initiated by the appearance of the translation of Goethe bespeaks the enthusiasm and the confidence of the collaborators. When their *Torquato Tasso* went to press, they had already begun work on Montesquieu's Persian Letters and proposed new translations of "Ariosto's *Orlando Furioso*, Machiavelli's *Mandragola*, selections from Leopardi, Tasso's *Jerusalem Delivered*, Lope de Vega's *Fuente Ovejuna* and *El Mejor Alcalde el Rey*, Calderon's *El Alcalde de Zalamea* and *El Majico Prodigioso*, Schiller's *Don Carlos*, Kleist's *Penthesilea*, selections from Hoelderlin,

Lermontov's *A Hero of Our Times*, selected colloquies of Erasmus, Diderot's *The Nun*, Beaumarchais' *The Marriage of Figaro*, and selections from French symbolist poets." Unfortunately, the first in the series proved also to be the last; Ben, on the vita which he prepared only months before his death, accounted for the abrupt demise of the plan in a terse and rather sour parenthetical note following the entry of the

translation of Goethe among his published works: "We were hoping that this would be the first in a series of translations, designed for use in courses in comparative literature, and that the series might prove to be the beginning of a University of Arkansas Press. We were unable to get financial support."

Undaunted, Ben and Duncan began exploring other outlets for their scholarly energies. In 1957 they submitted an article entitled "The Geography and History in *Nostromo*" to *Modern Philology*. Ben had written the piece, and Duncan warned him before he submitted it that the style left much to be desired. Ben grumbled and sent it off anyway. It was rejected. Duncan reworked the article, and they resubmitted it; it was published in 1958. After that incident, Ben somewhat grudgingly relinquished the job of final drafting to Duncan.

When the grand plan for a series of translations and the formation of a University of Arkansas Press was foiled, the two settled upon the project that eventually established for them international reputations as scholars: a biography of the 18th-century novelist Samuel Richardson. Duncan's major field of interest and expertise was 18th-century British literature (Ben once said, perhaps jokingly, perhaps not, that Duncan was the only person he knew who knew more about the 18th century than he did), so the work was his brain-child and his name appears first on the title page, as it had in the anthology, whereas Ben got top billing for the Goethe translation. By 1955 they had begun the preliminary work on the Richardson biography.

In the autumn of 1960, Ben took a leave of absence from the University to spend several months in England doing research for the book. His letters to Duncan during that time reflect some of the reasons why theirs was such a successful collaboration. Ben later said that Duncan was in many ways ideal as a research partner because, among other things, Duncan was much more patient and thorough than he, and the tone of some of the letters, that odd mixture of good nature and petulance of which Ben was singularly capable, suggests that Duncan sometimes had to push pretty hard to keep Ben after the information they wanted. Duncan, of course, since they were working in his field, was directing the research and knew where to go to find things, and, as the letters show, once Ben got on the trail of something, he was tireless in its pursuit. None of the letters from which the following excerpts are taken is dated, but the order can be fairly ascertained from their content:

> The records *are* in Mackworth, but no other S[samuel] R[ichardson] children there. At St. Alkmund's, the Derby parish bordering on Mackworth, the vicar had mentioned a Sara (the 1st daughter who died was Sarah) R. born in 1693 to S.R.--she's there, but not the fourth, the missing son.
> Against Mackworth's being our SR
> 1. The spelling of the name.
> 2. The missing son.
> For, besides father's name & date:
> Most important, the two Williams, leaving the second just the right age I think--I forgot to copy his marriage allegation & J. Wilde's--could you send me the information?

> You may remember that July 31 reminded Anne R. of much. 20 days is a likely delay from birth to baptism.
> The SR of Mackworth seems not to be a local--he was not married there or in the four Derby parishes included in a 15 vol. Derby Parish Register (marriages only--gave out after 73 parishes, but has Mackworth, st. Alkmund's, & some other neighboring ones) I found at Derby Public Library--the only SR marriage is a 1681 one at Smalley. He's not on a contemporary rent roll of the local manor, or in a 1670 Hearth tay(?) which includes Derby & Mackworth--only one R. in Derby, a "Ra: Richardson."
> On the whole I think it's ours, but damn the clerk's spelling. . . .
> I had no trouble seeing the Dagenham registers but papa & Benjy aren't there. I crawled under the piano & lifted the carpets, but found no slab for Willie.
> Everything else negative. No ads in the London Gazette 1680's besides the one Sale found. No helpful wills--I've almost finished there. I got Sale's records in Pub. Record Office, on printing, but nothing else. Have checked some more city parishes. The clerk of the chamberlain's court can't allow outsiders to see his records, but will check again--little hope. The armorers have lost one book, in the last war, bindings and freedoms together--you guess what dates. But if the clerk can find time he will, for a price, check the court books--I couldn't get at them. No slabs in st. Bot's or st. Katherine's.

**

This will be short as my finger's sore from 27 R. letters, in longhand, yesterday & today. Among other things I'm reminding the outstanding Derby vicars, but have no hope of a 100% return. I don't see any purpose in writing the parishes again that answered in 1955 but whose cards are lost--presumably they said what they had to say, & we can't get any very complete statistics in view of uncertainty about exactly how many parishes there were anyway. I've written a couple you didn't find, & I'm sure there are more. Anyway I think we have our entry. I'm going to Derby again the end of the week to search for the lost brother.

**

I do not have a note on John Leake's m[arriage], but if it's important I'll check it--you mean check the parish register? It's in the church . . . .

I gritted my teeth & went back to the Public Records Office, but there is no K.B.157. The Round Room is being repainted & things are even more confused. The librarian & I searched in the rubble for Fleet records, without success. If you want me to I'll try again when the painting's over, but it would help if you had the call no. I have no idea what you're going to do with it, since you don't know what it means.

The Derbyshire trip was a flop--no brother in the Derby churches, & three big boxes of miscellaneous records of the Munday family, owners of the local manor, had no reference to R. I did find the Fulham rate book--he moved into No. End in mid-1738.

If you get bored, you might glance at R to Young *Monthly Mag* May 24 1759 & to Lady B. June 5, '59, Forster XI, 259--doesn't the reference imply that the Warburghs died near London?

I'm finding nothing in the register or anywhere, & am ready to switch to checking references in the British Museum, which won't lead to anything but has to be done. Can't think of anything that will lead to any thing.

**

From Lichfield, where I've been checking bishop's transcripts of Derbyshire parishes--it seems they have most of them, so most of our work could have been done right here--but for a price, bishops (as you see) are only a little cheaper than portcullises . . . . No missing brother in any Derby parish or any other parish bordering on Mackworth.

In London, less happy--our idea of checking everything seems to have been a bust . . . . Most of my time now is in B[ritish] M[useum], & I only hope I can finish there—mainly on R's various newspapers. I've been to Oxford, tomorrow to a Mr. Stewart's house, who for some odd reason has got the Byfleet Court Roles. Is there anything else--urgent? I have to go once more to that damned P[ublic] R[ecords] O[office] about the *True Briton*. Guildhall & Som. House exhausted, so far as I know . . . .

"If you get bored and want something to do" here are some things to search for (I can't find them in B. M.):

The Citizen, 1739

Daily Gazetteer after 1744--it should go on at least till '47

Weekly Miscellany 1740-1

Daily Post of April 1734

Candid Review, and *Literary Reporter*, April, 1771

Daily Advertiser, Sept. 1750

(Is there another good periodical file in London besides BM?)

Also sales catalogues:-

      Walter T. Spencer, 1927

      Henry Sotheran & Co, 12 Nov 1904

      Francis Edwards, Dec. 1919

And the periodical (not collected) *Critical Review*, Jan.-Aug., 1756 (1st numbers).

You could have them all waiting for me, as a coming home present--just think, two months without R.!

Research is much less fun alone.

* * *

I will not quite finish checking the *Daily Journal*, having only one day more, but will get everything else on my list done. All city & east end parishes extant checked--no results. Did poppa & mamma go west or cross the river? or have I missed it, my eyes wandering in a huge parish. But I have not missed Benjy or the Warburgs. Where are they planted? . . .

Even Miss Wescomb didn't have the decency to be baptized at Kath. Coleman--her f. did get buried there. No one ever stuck to his damn parish.

So farewell to Sammy for a while--I'll rather miss him, & England too.

The work on Richardson engaged them for fifteen years, and the result was impressive. *Samuel Richardson: A Biography* appeared in 1971, published by the Clarendon Press, and is considered the definitive biography of Richardson.

Following the publication of the Richardson biography and an edition of his *Pamela*, a Riverside Edition for Houghton-Mifflin, in the same year, it was Ben's turn to choose their next project. Ben's primary interests had for many years been shifting to modern literature, and, after flirting with a number of his favorite 20th-century writers and works, he settled upon Ezra Pound's *Cantos*. As Duncan wrote in the *Paideuma* memorial, Ben made this choice "because of his admiration for Pound and especially The cantos and (in part) because he knew all the languages that Pound knew. Ben was, in fact, an ideal scholar to undertake this project."

One of the appeals of this project for Ben was the very challenge of it; *The Cantos*, along with James Joyce's *Finnegans Wake*, which Ben also considered as a subject for the project, are widely regarded as among the most imposing and difficult works ever written, and, when Ben decided upon *The Cantos* shortly before the Richardson biography appeared, no comprehensive guide to the work was available. When someone did publish a reader's guide to The Cantos in the mid-seventies, Ben, asked if its appearance would affect his work, replied that it would not, and when questioned why, said very simply, "Because ours will be so much better."

The tirelessness so evident in his letters regarding the work on Richardson redoubled in his pursuit of this project. He took a year's leave in 1969-70 to return to Harvard to do postdoctoral work in modern literature and the only language used in *The Cantos* that he didn't already know: Chinese. He also took advantage of his time there to study linguistics and transformational grammar, the latter of which he declared, not altogether disparagingly, to be "just as cute as it can be." Following his year at Harvard, he set aside a certain amount of time virtually every evening for the rest of his life to the study of Chinese.

In the Oxford lecture which Ben gave some months before his death, he described the work, which was projected to be completed in 1985:

> I'm trying to explain insofar as possible--I'll have to come back to the word "explain"; it's a trick word—The Cantos of Ezra Pound . . . . By "explain" one can mean several different things . . . . The process which I'm going to try to illustrate . . . is to try to zero in on what these things are about, why they are there, what kind of pattern they form, and then, beyond that, something about aesthetic method, about the attitudes that are being conveyed--notice I don't say

ideas; I think that's not really quite the right word for what you get out of a poem. Attitudes, feelings, values would come closer to it.

A glance at any one of the Cantos reveals how imposing a task Ben and Duncan had set for themselves; even to a relatively unlettered eye, that the work is rife with allusions becomes apparent, and Ben was intent upon identifying them all. On one of our trips to the West, he read several volumes of a medieval German history--in German--trying to track down a single reference, without success, as I recall. A letter to Duncan on stationery from the Grand Hotel in Rimini posted in July 1981, illustrates once again Ben's dogged determination to find things, as well as his wit:

Well, Broglio (original & copy) is where he ought to be, & I spent this morning on him. Unfortunately, the library closes at 1:15 (so far, that's true of every library this trip except the big one in Florence [where I found not MSS but some books & articles]). Whether I can finish tomorrow I don't know--wish I'd allowed another day here, but one more day now would be a Sunday, & therefore useless. I can try to arrange a photocopy, but have only moderate hope of that. I may have to cut Rome entirely & stay over Monday *or* Tuesday. Hate to go too fast & miss things. No doubt P. used Broglio. I'll hold this letter open & let you know tomorrow what I decide. In Modena, I found, as I was pretty sure I would, the Mandates (p. 110)--P. as with Monte(?] dei ~. also used a published source which I have. Unexpected, one missing line in the Este (p. 113), two requests by P. for longish lists of documents which turned out to be useless (hopes dashed & partly restored by) "sed et universus in[?]" (p. 130)--building of Modena cath., a surprise. In Florence, the long letter on pp. 28-9 (expected--F. also used a published source) & (unexpected) the letter to Giovanni on p. 30, ll. 26-32. In Mary de R's translation of Cantos I-XXX is a facsimile of the Pisanello letter, said to be in the Ambrosian in Milan, so that's hopeful. It takes a good while ever to find where things are & how to locate them. I've probably missed things, but I've been at it every minute libraries are open. To the right of the door as you enter San Zeno is a relic of Theodoric, who if memory serves has an empty tomb at Ravenna--can't waste library time checking here. After libraries close, I have lots of time--to eat & to read, mostly. If the slave market in Charleston is still open, please buy me one with fluent Italian & a course in paleography, since I'll probably have to return. Fra Angelicos (& a __ [?] of Lemelle d'Este) were easy at Cortona, but everyone at Sanse pulao[?] looked blank about four metal bishops--not in museum or cathedral, & small towns don't have tourist offices.

Well, I couldn't finish so I'll have to cut out Rome. I'd better do all I can with Broglie while I have him--don't trust a photocopy.

Meanwhile, Duncan was also at work in the States, as a second letter attests, written from Castel Nouvel, Varetz, France, where Ben stayed several days in early August of the same summer:

Congratulations on finding the Frobenius ref. (don't worry about the headless lines--I have them in a book, but thought since they were in Cantos with water & drawings they'd be from the same source). And I'm sure you found just what we need on Leo D. You've done better than I have since Rimini--& even there Broglie was rather disappointing, still a good many missing Malatesta lines. Milan was infuriating, though I did find a couple of minor things at the Ambrosian. The library in the Breda never heard of Carioli--I searched not only author but also subject files (Italy has no title catalog) with the help of two sweet but rather bewildered young people. And I failed to find the Pisanello letter, though I went through their complete list of MSS--two days looking at anything dated XV cent., in Italian. I could have missed it in the six huge volumes. Only catalog is by authors, & according to the successor of Pius XI (who helped P(ound)) not all letters are in it under author. I did find most of the locations near Rapallo[?] & got the prison camp located pretty well with the help of Pisan tourist office. I saw the tapestries at Chaise Dreis(?) & though I didn't climb up to Montsegus(?) (1 km. almost straight up, stairs along a cliff) I found a good guidebook with pictures. Ex [?] is still closed to public, & the man in the tourist office never heard of a well. Damn.

Ben pointed out in his Oxford lecture that many people see research as presenting two possibilities: being "brilliantly original" or being a drudge. He felt this was a false dichotomy, but since research is often viewed in this way, he characterized his work on Pound thus: "I guess I'd say on the whole on the drudgery side, but not altogether." Certainly, sifting through several boxes of miscellaneous records or poring over a six-volume index of documents in search of some small fact may seem like drudgery, but for Ben it was perhaps like nothing so much as panning for gold. Beyond the pleasure he took in discovery were two other aspects of his character that made him the quintessential researcher: he had the persistence of a true sleuth, and he loved games.

He played games energetically, earnestly, seriously (but not solemnly), and with absolute integrity. One of his favorites was the license-plate game, which we played on all of our trips west. He made the rules: no plate could be counted unless at least two people had seen it. We discovered an emendation to the rules one evening in Santa Fe. We had arrived mid-afternoon, and Ben had gone to his room while Johnny, Jack Butler, and I went out exploring. We found a car with a Massachusetts plate--one we were missing--parked in a two-hour zone in front of a church at least three blocks from our hotel. We told Ben about it several hours later when we all met in the bar of La Fonda before dinner. He already had a margarita in hand when he got the news. "Where exactly was it?" he wanted to know. We told him, but assured him that the chances of its still being there were very slender. He agreed, but we could see that he was growing restless.

Suddenly he got up. "I'll be right back," he said and headed at a brisk pace toward the door.

He returned in about ten minutes, nodding with visible satisfaction. "It was still there," he said as he sat down to enjoy his drink. The rules were tacitly emended: two people had to see the license plate, and one of them had to be Ben. We eventually had to stand firm against him even on that; he got a little miffed at us for refusing to count one that only he had seen--happily, we later saw another like it.

During one of his sojourns at Harvard he played the license plate game all year on his own, confining it to the city limits of Cambridge. When he left Cambridge to return to Fayetteville, he had recorded every U.S. plate but one: Arkansas. The one on his own car was the only one he ever saw, but he couldn't count it: it was one of the rules of his game.

Such integrity in so small a thing mirrors all his endeavors, including his scholarship. One senses something solid and trustworthy about everything he did.

When Ben died, Duncan continued the work in the hope of finishing it and engaged David Strain, who at the time was doing graduate work at Fayetteville and had been close to Ben for the last two years of his life, to help him with the monumental task of sorting out, transcribing, and making sense of Ben's notes. Tragically, Duncan's health, which had not been good for some time, soon failed him as well; he suffered a debilitating stroke within a year of his dearest friend's death. He fought back gamely, and continued his work both as a teacher and as a scholar until his death in April 1986.

Between 1977 and the time of Ben's death, Ben and Duncan had published nineteen articles relating to Pound, and five others had been accepted for publication. To date these are the only publically available results of their thirteen years of research. The mantle of responsibility for the Pound book--and a heavy mantle it was indeed--passed to Mr. Strain, who at this writing is completing his doctoral work at Harvard, a labor that has necessarily precluded any further work on *The Cantos*.

The hundreds of pages of notes that Ben made over the years for the Pound book become increasingly cryptic and hasty in the later work. They provide one of the few hints that he may have foreseen that he was not going to live his full three-score and ten. An urgency betrayed by an uncharacteristic superficiality in the last notes suggests at least some fear that he might not live to complete the work. His uneasiness was exacerbated by increasing difficulties with his eyes which resulted in his having cataract surgery in January before his death in April. He continued working, however, to the last, as Duncan Eaves' memorial bears witness:

> It had been his custom to come to my house around nine in the evening, when we would work together on The Cantos; but that evening when I telephoned him shortly after nine and received no answer, I drove to his house and found him seated in a chair, a volume of *The Cantos*, the latest issue of *Paideuma*, and various notes on Pound on a table beside him, and an unlit cigarette in his mouth. A folder of matches had dropped from his hand beside his chair. Were it not for the cigarette, he appeared simply to have fallen asleep.

The time of death was estimated to have been about six in the evening on Thursday, April 21, 1983. At about that time, some two hundred miles south of Fayetteville, a young man named Jay Curlin, also a Fort Smith native, who had met Ben and was anticipating studying under him the next fall, was presenting a paper, the result of an excellent honors project on Richard Wilbur which he had done under the direction of Johnny Wink. One of the poems that Jay discussed that evening was "The Undead," in which the essential emptiness of the vampire's "thirst for mere survival" is briefly contrasted with the value of quiet lives of integrity and endeavor:

> ... Thinking
> Of a thrush cold in the leaves
> Who has sung his few summers truly,
> Or an old scholar resting his eyes at last,
> We cannot be much impressed with vampires,
> Colorful though they are.

Chapter Four

"He was not self-centered but broad in his interests, catholic in his open-heartedness and engaging and winning in his warm spirit of fellowship."

These words appeared in the *Fort Smith Southwestern* in an editorial lamenting the death of Ben Drew Kimpel--not on April 22, 1983, but on October 10, 1918; Ben Drew Kimpel, Sr., died almost exactly a month before his son's third birthday. Ben rarely spoke of his family; most of his students knew that he was from Fort Smith, that he had been devoted to his mother, and that he had a sister living in Fort Smith, but even those close to him knew very little more. He obviously had a considerable income apart from his salary: teachers at the University of Arkansas, even if they are full professors and unmarried, do not have the wherewithal to travel about the globe at will, lend or give large sums of money to various people, and build comfortable homes to their own specifications. Legend had it that his family "owned half of downtown Fort Smith." It was not all so grandiose as that, but, certainly, Ben had his resources, thanks to the talents and industry of his father and the foresight and good business sense of his mother.

Ben Drew Kimpel, Sr., was the oldest of the four children of David and Beulah A. Kimpel of Dermott, Arkansas. D. Kimpel, as David (or, more frequently, Dave) Kimpel habitually signed himself, was born of Jewish parents on January 16, 1858, in Wurzburg, Germany, and immigrated to the United states in 1873-according to one source, to avoid conscription in the army. In 1881, he married Beulah Godwin (b.1867), and they had settled in Dermott by the time of Ben Drew's birth on November 20, 1883. Dave Kimpel's business interests in Dermott included real estate, a mercantile store, and a partnership in the Lephieuw Cotton Gin. In a biographical sketch of Charles F. Wells appearing in an 1890 history of southern Arkansas, Kimpel is mentioned as a partner in the general merchandise establishment of Morris, Kimpel & Wells, having an inventory "valued at about $5, 000 or $6, 000." Beulah Kimpel also had a millinery shop in Dermott which she purchased in 1891 and operated with one Daisy Kimpel, whose relationship to the family I have been unable to determine.

Dave Kimpel, who, incidentally, was blind in one eye and wore a patch over it, has been described by the nephew of one of his business associates as "very aggressive," and the numbers of dealings recorded between 1884 and his death in 1929 in the Chicot County

Books of Deeds attest to the accuracy of that assessment, at least insofar as his commercial interests were concerned. Otherwise, the frequency with which the Kimpel name appears in the Dermott News after its inception in 1910 indicates the prominence he and his family enjoyed in the business, civic, and social life of the community, and his position as a "town father" is shown in everything from locals reporting that "D. Kimpel got a Victor Victrola for Christmas" (12/28/11) or that he and his wife had departed for California with friends "in the Kimpel Oldsmobile" (7/3/19) to the paper's quoting him as one of the town sages during the 1916 flood: "D. Kimpel says he has lived here 34 years and has never known the town to be in the slightest danger from floodwater, nor does he believe such a thing possible, much less probable" (2/3/16). The last quotation may have caused him some embarrassment nine years later when the floods of late April and early May 1927 left downtown Dermott, including his home and business, under several feet of water. He was elected one of the directors of the Bank of Dermott in 1926 and became its vice-president, a position which he resigned early in 1929 because of his failing health. He died Tuesday morning, May 21, 1929, following surgery at the Baptist Hospital in Memphis, Tennessee, and his funeral, attended by, among many others, his fourteen-year-old grandson to whom, more than a decade earlier, he had read silent-movie captions, was held May 23 at the Methodist Church in Dermott. The following is from a tribute to Mr. Kimpel printed in the *Dermott News*, May 30, 1929:

> Coming to Dermott a mere youth with practically nothing of material possessions, Mr. Kimpel through his initiative, industrious habits, perseverance and good business judgment gradually became one of the substantial, outstanding figures of the community. He acquired extensive farming and mercantile interests. At the time of his death he was senior partner of the firm of Kimpel & Bynum, general merchants, and Kimpel & Lephieuw, ginners and cotton buyers. He was also a director of the Dermott Grocery & Commission Company, and until a short time ago was vice-president of the Bank of Dermott.
>
> He was highly regarded by the entire community, and held an especial place in the esteem of the negroes, who regarded him as their friend and benefactor.

In Dave Kimpel's will, probated June, 15, 1929, he stipulated that his son, Ernie, the trustee of his estate, "as soon as same comes into his hands, first pay to my grandson, Ben Drew Kimpel, the son of Ben D. Kimpel, for his own use and benefit, the sum of five hundred ($500.00) dollars." The remainder of his estate was to be held in trust for his two daughters and his two other grandchildren.

The Kimpels had four children, Ben Drew (b.1883), Bertha (b.1886), Leonora (b.1889), and Ernest B. (b.1895), and they also provided a home for Beulah's younger half-sister, Letitia Cecil, after the death of her mother.

Ben Drew Kimpel, Sr., completed his public school education in Dermott, and enrolled in the University of Arkansas, where he studied for three years. He was admitted to the bar in 1906, following his graduation from the Columbia University school of law on June 6, 1906. He joined the Fort smith law firm of Col. T. P. Winchester and W. R. Martin the same year, and continued his study of law under them for two years before entering into a partnership with Harry P. Daily to form the law firm Kimpel & Daily in January, 1909.

Col. Winchester is quoted as saying of the young Mr. Kimpel, "I well remember when Ben first came to our office. He told me that he was not seeking money, but knowledge of the law. He said he had a 'smattering' of law but said he realized he was incapable of practicing for a livelihood. I took great liking to the young man, as I soon learned he bore great promise. He was an apt student and ready to learn.

"The only vacation I ever had in my life," Colonel Winchester continues, "was due to Ben. He insisted that I take a leave of absence, and I was so impressed with his insistence that I finally consented. He was a splendid young man, possessed great executive ability, a hard worker and loyal to the core."

When he entered into a partnership with Mr. Daily, the young lawyer's newly established practice flourished, eventually growing to be one of the leading firms in western Arkansas, and he increasingly involved himself in public and civic affairs. on April 11, 1912, he married Gladys Crane (it may amuse those readers who witnessed over the years the misspelling of our subject's surname to know that Ben's father's name appeared on his marriage certificate as 'Ben D. Kimple'); their only child, Ben Drew Kimpel, Jr., was born in Fort Smith on November 6, 1915.

Late in September of 1918, Ben, Sr., who was at the time the Sebastian County chairman of the Arkansas United War Work campaign, travelled to Little Rock for a statewide meeting of that organization. There he was stricken with Spanish influenza from which thousands were dying in the United States' worst epidemic of the century. He returned to Fort Smith, where he died two weeks later of pneumonia on October 9, 1918, six weeks before his thirty-fifth birthday. The following excerpts are from articles appearing in the *Dermott News*, the *Fort Smith Times Record*, and the *Fort Smith Southwestern*:

BRIGHT CAREER OF BEN KIMPEL ENDS BY DEATH
Tributes to Ben Kimpel

"One of the leaders of the community. The city [of Fort Smith] has suffered a great loss."--John c. Gardner, president Arkansas Valley Bank.

"The city [of Fort Smith] has suffered an irreparable loss. His memory will be cherished by his legion of friends."--Judge Jos. M. Hill.

"A man in whom you could place every confidence, a keen lawyer and a splendid young fellow."--Thos. B. Pryor, former chairman Democratic County Central Committee.

"Fort Smith has sustained a hard blow. He was a natural born leader, an indefatigable worker who gave much for the benefit of his city."--Ray Gill, secretary Business Men's Club.

"Fort Smith loses a splendid type of citizenship in the passing of Ben Kimpel."--Arch Monro, mayor.

. . . The death of Mr. Kimpel brought sorrow to all Fort Smith. While it was known that he had been desperately ill for the past few days, his friends hoped his strong constitution, his wonderful vitality and power of resistance would aid in the fight his physicians were making for his life, and that he would recover.

. . . In the death of the brilliant young attorney Fort Smith has sacrificed another hero to the great world war, for Mr. Kimpel gave his life in the cause of freedom quite as bravely as do those soldiers who fall on the field of battle. He has been prominent in every war measure since the United States entered the war, working with the enthusiasm of youth and the patriotism of the true American.

. . . All day Wednesday and Thursday messages of condolence came to the stricken home from hundreds of sorrowing friends in the city and all over the state, and a special car was required to take the floral pieces to Forest Park, where Mr. Kimpel was laid to rest at 5 o'clock.

. . . For the first time since the stars and stripes have floated over the county courthouse the city's flag is at half mast. The flag was lowered Wednesday evening in honor of Mr. Kimpel, and was kept at half mast until after the funeral services Thursday afternoon.

. . . As a community Fort Smith deplores the untimely death of Ben D. Kimpel. Much more than most of the younger men of affairs in this city had he dedicated his time and his talent and his matchless energy to the advancement of all our public and community interests. He was not self-centered but broad in his interests, catholic in his open-heartedness and engaging and winning in his warm spirit of fellowship. He seemed to have before him one of the most useful and honorable careers, one that promised much to the city so long as he maintained his citizenship with us. No young man among us had so closely and largely identified himself with every community interest.

Balfour D. Crane was born October 26, 1856, in Hernando, Mississippi. His father, the Reverend William Carey Crane, was instrumental in the establishment of the Mississippi Baptist Female College in Hernando in 1851, serving as its first president, and, according to one of his biographers, "turned down calls to the presidency of five male colleges and six female colleges to remain in Mississippi," where, in 1857, he founded the Semple-Broadus College at Center Hill (DeSoto county) . In 1859, the family moved from Mississippi to Mt. Lebanon, Louisiana, where William Carey Crane served one year as the president of the State University before moving on to Independence, Texas, to become the president of Baylor University, a position he held from 1863 to 1885. Balfour came to Little Rock in the late 1870s or early 1880s, moving to Fort Smith in 1885. In 1888 he married Elizabeth (Mattie) Davis (b.1866), the daughter of Sarah J. and Pleasant R. Davis. The P.R. Davis family had come to Fort Smith from North Carolina and Tennessee soon after the Civil War and by the 1880s had established itself, as one journalist described it, as "one of the foremost families of the south and Southwest."

Crane's first connection in Fort Smith was with John C. Hill and J. S. Skipwith, cotton brokers; he left that firm in a few years to become associated with his father-in-law's business, Reynolds-Davis & Company, later the Reynolds-Davis Grocery Company, of which he was president at the time of his death in 1928. In 1904, he formed with his brother-in-law, John Witherspoon, the Fort Smith Coffee Company. From 1923 to 1927, the Cranes lived in Fayetteville, where he was the president and manager of the Ozark Grocer Company. He was a director of the Southern Wholesale Grocers' Association and a president of the Arkansas Wholesale Grocers' Association. He was also very active in the civic affairs of Fort Smith and was one of the leaders of the Fort Smith Chamber of Commerce, serving two terms as president of that organization. He died on June 1, 1928, four days after having undergone an emergency appendectomy.

Gladys Crane--whose father insisted that her name be pronounced glay-dis--was born in Fort Smith in January 1889, the oldest child and only daughter of Balfour and Mattie crane. She and her brothers, Davis (b.1890), B.D., Jr. (Dorsett--b.1893), and Carey (b.1894) attended public school in Fort Smith, where all of them eventually settled down with their families. Well educated (she attended Hollins College in Virginia), cultured, unassuming, and strikingly beautiful, Gladys must have been much sought-after by the young men of Northwest Arkansas before her marriage at the age of twenty-three to Ben D. Kimpel, and the union of two such luminaries of the community was undoubtedly one of the social highlights of the spring of 1912 in Fort Smith. Relatives have suggested that the six and a half years of marriage that Ben and Gladys had were very happy ones for both of them and that, despite her naturally resilient nature, she was very nearly brought down by her grief when he died.

Gladys Kimpel invested her late husband's earnings in the construction of an office building known as the Flatiron Building in downtown Fort Smith, and with the city's growth, it proved to be a very wise and lucrative investment. Rents from the property provided an ample income, much of which was either used for her son's education or placed in trust for him.

Five years after her first husband's death, on July 16, 1923, she married William E. Porter, a handsome young man who had come to Fort Smith after the war from Shelbyville, Indiana, to manage a branch of the Porter Mirror Glass Company, which his father, Enos Porter, of Shelbyville, had established in Fort Smith. In the summer of 1924, the Por-ers and eight-year-old Ben Kimpel moved to Los Angeles, where William had the responsibility of setting up another glass factory for his father. On December 19, 1924, their daughter, Elizabeth, was born.

By the spring of 1925, the strain which the organization of the new plant involved became too much for young Porter, and the family returned to Fort smith. In May, William entered a hospital in Battle Creek, Michigan, where he died in July of 1925. Gladys and the children remained for the rest of her life at the Porter residence at 901 South 21st Street in Fort Smith. She never remarried. Ben had no memory of his father but remembered his step-father well, and whenever he spoke of him, it was with fondness.

From all evidence, Gladys Crane was a remarkable woman-attractive, intelligent, sensitive, and energetic. Her family's wealth and social position seem to have had on her character none of the unfortunate effects that one sometimes observes among members of the privileged classes. She has been described as "very down-to-earth" and "unaffected"; she did not employ servants, although she had grown up with servants in her parents' home. She, however, preferred to do the housework and especially the cooking herself. She and Ben maintained their ties with his father's family and visited Dermott at least once a year until Ben went off to school. On these visits they usually stayed with Beulah Kimpel's half-sister, Mrs. J. O. Hoffman, born Letitia Cecil (1880), primarily because of the warm friendship that had developed between Mrs. Hoffman and Gladys, but also because, according to Mrs. Hoffmann's daughter, Virginia Hodges, Gladys had come to feel not altogether comfortable in the Kimpel home on account of the servants. Dave and Beulah Kimpel employed cooks, gardeners, maids, and even a chauffeur, and Gladys no longer felt quite at ease having other people do what she not only preferred to do but also enjoyed doing herself. She particularly loved to cook, and Mrs. Hodges had warm memories of the great fun her mother and Gladys had during those long, pleasant hours in Mrs. Hoffman's kitchen.

Mrs. Hoffmann was closer in age to her nephew than to her sister, and she and Gladys, alike in temperament and sharing common interests and tastes, were drawn together into a close and lasting bond. The friendship spanned forty years, from the time Gladys married Mrs. Hoffmann's nephew Ben in 1912 until Gladys's death. The two travelled to California together by train in 1919 or 1920, accompanied by the four- or five-year-old Ben and Mrs. Hoffman's daughter, Virginia.

Gladys was determined to help her son become a citizen of the world through both an exceptional education and extensive travel, but this determination was not high-handed; she apparently tried to assure that paths remained open and rich and enticing so that Ben's native curiosity and the pleasure he naturally took from learning would lead him as far along them as he could or wanted to go. She was sensitive to his inclinations and encouraged him to make his own decisions while he was still a very small child. Virginia Hoffman Hodges recalls that on the train to California when Ben was only four or five he ordered his own meals, although once he appeared to be rather tired of being asked what he wanted and told the waiter he wanted "fried elephant ears."

On Sunday, March 30, 1952, travelling alone, Gladys Porter left Hot Springs, where she had been on a month-long visit, to return to Fort Smith. She was apparently killed instantly when her car crossed the center line and struck head-on an eastbound vehicle on highway 270 about twenty miles west of Hot Springs. Ben, who was at Harvard doing post-doctoral work in preparation for joining the faculty at the University in Fayetteville, was notified of the tragedy by his brother-in-law, Charles Warner. His mother's death was the most difficult thing Ben ever bore. He credited her with having been the greatest influence on his life, and, although he rarely spoke of his feelings for her, they were clear: in the last ten years of his life he often revisited places he had first traveled to with her, and hers was the only photograph ever displayed in his house--it rested on his desk in the lower section of his great room until he died. Whenever he spoke of her, his voice was filled with a certain warmth, respect, and admiration, so that what he said did not reveal the depth of his feeling for her so much as how he said it.

How much his having come from people involved in business and the law may have influenced Ben is pure speculation, but he unquestionably possessed many of the qualities which are associated with success in commercial and legal affairs. He was extremely practical, thorough, methodical, and well-organized; he managed his finances very well; he got along with many different sorts of people; he was a tireless worker with a strong sense of duty; and his gift for expressing ideas clearly, succinctly, and persuasively would be the envy of anyone charged with arguing a case or selling a product. He said of himself and others have often said of him that he could argue either side of any question with equal facility and vigor, so that had he stayed with law as a vocation, it might have proven a good choice.

It is perhaps appropriate, after a look at Ben's family background, to address the fact that he did not perpetuate his line--at least, not to the knowledge of anyone consulted in the research for this book. Ben died a bachelor, and, according to Duncan Eaves, he only proposed marriage once in his life--to a woman whom everyone who knew her has described as Ben's equal in both intelligence and wit. When Ben asked her to marry him— they were both at Chapel Hill and Ben was shortly to receive his Ph.D. and enlist in the Army--she told him simply that she was in love with another of his friends, whom she later married; Ben remained friends with them for the rest of his life. Duncan told me that Ben accepted the refusal in a very matter-of-fact manner and never spoke of it again except to say, many years later, "It's a good thing Margaret didn't marry me; we'd have killed each other." Ben told us, on one of our trips to the West, only that he had made a decision fairly early in his life. "I knew I couldn't do *everything* I wanted to do," he said, "and so I chose not to marry and have a family." Once he made this decision, he seemed never to look back; in this, as in other choices he had made in his life, he appeared to have escaped the curse of regret.

Asked whether Ben had ever been involved with a woman after he joined the faculty in Fayetteville, Claude Faulkner responded, "Not that I know of--but there were plenty of women who wanted to be involved with him." He mentioned one who lamented, "I'd be glad to take him on any terms--but he doesn't have any terms!"

Many people have expressed a certain sadness that Ben left no progeny, and certainly, the only result of the conjunction of the Kimpel and Crane lines being what it was, such regrets are understandable. But however we may speculate about what his life might have been had he married, it is difficult to imagine anything very much finer than his life as it was.

CHAPTER FIVE

From the time Ben was a little tyke ordering fried elephant ears for dinner on a California-bound train, one of the great passions of his life was travel; as he wrote in the Harvard Class of 1937 40th Anniversary Report in 1977, "My main diversion continues to be travel, whenever I can get free of duties as chairman of the English department." It is unlikely that many who read the final clause in that statement would have recognized its tone, which was, I assure you, one of extreme irritation. Of the many things about being chairman that annoyed Ben, one of the most irksome was that it interfered with his freedom to travel. Before he was chairman, however, not only his summers, but also the Christmas and spring holidays were almost always devoted to trips; hardly would the last bell have rung before he would be off, by car, by plane, by boat, or by train--when that was still possible--to places most people only dream of visiting or to those that it never occurs to most people to visit. Lyell Behr has reported that "Ben is only the second person I ever met who had been to Ulan Bator." For much of his life, one of his ambitions was to visit every country, or, at the very least, as he once told Professor Behr, "to see every place of consequence in the world."

A thorough account of Ben's life as a traveler, even if it omitted all of his other activities, would fill several volumes the size of this one. In the fall of 1980, he made the following list of the major trips he had taken each year, beginning with the first one of which he had clear memories, a trip to Toronto with his mother when he was six years old. He did not list earlier excursions because, -although he knew about them, his memories of them were somewhat jumbled and the impressions vague or isolated.

    1922—Toronto
    1923—Fayetteville
    1924—Los Angeles
    1925—Winslow, AR
    1926—Northern Michigan
    1927—Europe
    1928—New England, Quebec

1929—Culver, Canadian Rockies; Cuba, Panama (wntr)
1930—Europe
1931—Little Rock, Creede, Denver, Nebraska
1932—Santa Fe, Creede
1933—Chicago
1934—Creede, Mesa Verde
1935—Mexico
1936—Yellowstone, Glacier, Utah, Carlsbad, San Antonio; Florida (spr)
1937—Scandinavia, England, Germany
1938—Massachusetts
1939—Greece, Italy
1940—Kentucky, Louisiana
1941—California
1942—Little Rock
1943—Mississippi
1944—England, France
1945—Belgium, Netherlands, Germany
1946—American Northwest, Austria
1947—Czechoslovakia, Austria
1948—Switzerland, Prague, Hungary; England (Xmas)
1949—Poland
1950—Washington, D.C.
1951—Maine, Canada
1952—Austria, Italy, London
1953—Las Vegas, San Francisco
1954—Spain, Italy
1955—England, Germany
1956—West Indies, Guatemala; (?)El Paso, Mexico (spr)
1957—Around the world, Yugoslavia
1958—Belgian Congo, S. and E. Africa, Egypt, Jordan, Israel
1959—Berlin, Poland, USSR, Greece, Sicily; Yucatan, Paleopal(?) (spr)
1960—Australia, New Zealand, Hawaii, Tahiti, South Seas; El Salvador, Santa Rosa de Copan (Honduras) (spr)
1961—England, Scotland, Austria, Egypt; Mexico (spr)
1962—Syria, Morocco; Iceland, Scandinavia, Bayreuth, St. Maarten
1963—South America

1964—Bremen, Brittany, Spain, Portugal
1965—Around the world 1966—North Italy, Alsace, South Italy, Malta, Tunis
1967—England
1968—USSR, Mongolia, Balkans, Pyrenees, Finland; Guatemala (spr)
1969—West Africa, West Indies; New England; Nicaragua (spr)
1970—England, Scotland, E. Germany, Netherlands, France, Switzerland; East Coast, VA, NC (spr); Guatemala, Mexico (Xmas)
1971—S. and E. Africa, London; Iraq, Ethiopia (Xmas)
1972—N. France, Ireland, Wales; s. France, N. Italy; Antarctica (Xmas)
1973—Arizona, California Japan, SE Asia, Indonesia; London, New York (Xmas)
1974—S. France, N. Spain, Italy, Sardinia, Belgium; Mexico (spr); Austria, London (Xmas)
1975—Big Bend, Santa Fe; Glacier, Isle Royal; China
1976—Utah; England, Wales; Norway to Munich
1977—New Haven, Cambridge; Ontario
1978—Grand Tetons, Black Hills; Italy, France, Germany (?)
1979—New Haven
1980—El Paso; Italy, France, London

He kept a record of many of his travels in two oversized scrapbooks, approximately twenty by twenty-four inches, each containing about fifty leaves; the pages are filled with the maps of every state in the United States and almost every country in the world. Over each map he traced a gridwork of lines representing routes that he had taken to various spots in the state or country, and these markings reveal that, when Ben said he had been to a place, he had indeed been there. On one of several maps of England, for example, virtually every route, major and minor, in all regions of the country, is marked with the characteristic heavy blue or black tracings.

He took organized tours only when it was absolutely necessary, as was the case, for example, with his trip to China in 1975; otherwise he planned his trips himself or with the aid of a travel agent in New York recommended to him by one of his favorite traveling companions, Jessie O'Kelly, or, for less demanding itineraries, agents in Northwest Arkansas or Little Rock. Jessie also planned some of his trips, including his first trip around the world.

One trip that the New York agent arranged for him was the one to Africa in 1971. The summer is not at all a good time to tour southern and eastern Africa because of the rains; as a consequence, most tours are scheduled for more agreeable times of the year. Ben insisted that he could not go unless he went in the summer, and, despite all arguments against the idea, was determined to make the trip. All of the necessary arrangements were made, including the engagement of various guides who transported him by jeep or private plane to game preserves and other areas of the countries that he could not reach on his own. It was on one of these excursions that the jeep in which he, the driver-guide, and one other passenger were riding got hopelessly stuck in the mud. The guide, seeing the situation would require aid, was about to go off for help when the other passenger said he was sure he could get them out and took the wheel. The result of his efforts was to turn the jeep over, and Ben's collarbone and several of his ribs were broken in the mishap. He finally got to a small village where there happened to be a French doctor, who did the best he could with his limited supplies and put Ben in a body cast so that he would be able to make the trip home.

Although, when the cast was removed in Fort Smith, he had several very painful lesions, Ben never had anything but praise for the French doctor, and on many occasions during his long recovery wished that he still had the body cast. He maintained that without the cast the trip home would have been excruciating if not impossible because of the pain, which was considerable even with the cast.

So far as I know, the African venture was the only one of his voyages to end or be interrupted because of an injury or serious illness. He always enjoyed remarkably good health and, although he often traveled over dangerous terrain and was conveyed on everything from camels and jeeps to rafts and single engine planes, was never involved in another serious accident. He also drove thousands and thousands of miles himself, but he was an excellent driver--the best I have ever ridden with--and, to my knowledge, was never in a wreck.

His distaste for organized tours was not an indication of his strong independence only, but of other things about him as well. For one thing, the idea of being herded hither and thither on a tour, waiting for stragglers, and then being rushed to keep up with a timetable not of his own making was detestable to Ben, and, even more important, he wanted to choose his own company when he traveled; when asked about why he decided to arrange as he had the African trip on which he was injured, he replied that he had wanted a real experience and didn't want to go on any trip where a lot of women were loaded in a jeep and somebody would say, "There's a giraffe," and they would nod and say, "Mm-hmm."

Since traveling was one of the greatest pleasures of his life, he naturally preferred to do it with companions who liked to do and see the same kinds of things he did, who were interesting to be with and could provide good conversation and good fun, and who, like him, were both leisurely and prompt. Jessie O'Kelly has told an anecdote which not only reveals one of the many differences between Ben and Duncan but also probably goes a long way toward explaining why, even though Duncan was his oldest and dearest friend, Ben rarely traveled with him, relatively speaking. But Jessie, Ben, and Duncan once took a trip to New Orleans and Biloxi, returning to Arkansas by way of Natchez, and in the evening, Ben would ask them what time they wanted to leave the next morning. "Now I don't care," Ben would say, "what time we leave; I just want to know when." Duncan's response was often, "Well, why don't we try for nine o'clock?" And Ben would say, "Damn it, I don't want to try for anything; I don't want to get up and sit around for an hour waiting for you. It seems to me any man your age, in forty-something years, ought to have learned how long it takes him to dress!"

Another very important reason for Ben's distaste for tours was that their itineraries often stipulate where and for how long meals might be taken. That would not have done for Ben at all. Meals were for him among the high points of every day of travel. When I was in graduate school, I heard tales of a famous "eating tour" of France that he and Jessie O'Kelly were reputed to have taken one summer. The story had it that they first located in the Michelin guide all the three-star restaurants where they wanted to eat and then planned the rest of their trip around them. I asked Jessie about this story; she laughed engagingly and said, "They were all eating tours!"

Mrs. O'Kelly was a member of the English faculty at Fayetteville when Ben arrived in 1952, and one of the splendid services she performed for the students and the University was to take groups of students to Europe in the summer, alternating summers with a friend with whom she also ran a small travel agency. The group would tour for six weeks together, and then the students would study for six weeks in England, France, or Spain, during which time Jessie was free to travel on her own. In the late fifties Ben began to join her. France and England were the countries they toured the most often, but they also traveled together in Scandinavia, Scotland, Italy, and Spain.

Ben and Jessie were ideal traveling companions. The adjectives that describe Jessie--attractive, gracious, good-natured, witty, intelligent, learned, unaffected--recall descriptions of Ben's favorite and most frequent traveling companion, his mother. Jessie has also given a succinct explanation of why they got on so well: "We both liked to see the same things, and both of us liked to be on time, and both of us liked to do the thing in a leisurely way--so that worked out just fine. And his good humor just never flagged; that was one of the pleasantest things about traveling with him. He was never hurried, and he was never late, and he was never flurried; you don't find many people like that."

Some of their trips as Jessie has described them provide a glimpse into the richness of experience they shared over the years:

1962, Scandinavia: That was the only time we took a packaged tour; we didn't have too much time for Denmark, so we took the Fairytale Tour, which lasts only three days. It starts at Copenhagen; then you can go back to Copenhagen if you want to. If you don't, you can get off at one of those ports and take a boat to either Norway or Sweden. We took a boat to Norway; we spent two or three days in Oslo and then went by train across country and took a coastal vessel which serves all the little fishing villages along the coast of Norway; they bring food in and take away mostly fish. We just loved it because you stop at every little town, every single little fishing village because that is their only communication with the outside world. The mountains are right behind, and there are no roads coming through, so they depend on these boats to bring everything they need and to take away whatever they want to sell.

They let us get off, and then they blew a whistle when they wanted us back on the boat. The towns were so little that we could walk all through them. The children were so curious--they saw so few outside people--that they followed us around most of the time.

We went all the way up to the Russian border, where you could go all the way back on the boat or you could take a bus across that hump and meet the boat on the coast, which is what we did. We nearly froze to death. This was in August--we really should have gone earlier.

The bus would stop and just let people on wherever somebody was standing by the side of the road, and they let them bring the dogs on, too. We passed one poor man up who kept waving, and the bus driver just drove on. Everybody began to say, "There's somebody there," and the driver said, "I know; I know that man. He can't get on my bus; he smells too bad." Most of them smelled fairly bad, so we thought this man really must be bad.

We spent the night at what was really a summer hotel, because these busses didn't run in the winter, and that is where we nearly froze to death. There was no heat, and it was a frame building--just one thickness, and no heat at all. That was a cold night, I'm telling you; I put my coat and everything else I possessed on top of the cover.

1972, France: It was a very interesting trip when we went to Proust's house. It took quite a bit of doing on Ben's part beforehand. They don't have any money in that little town; it's off the beaten paths, and nobody goes there, but they have an organization called the Friends of Proust, and Ben found out about that--I don't know how or where, but he did--and found that you had to write ahead, and so he did. We found the house in the town and the little old Frenchman who had charge of everything. He was very apologetic; he said, "We just don't have any money; we can't do what we want to do, what we ought to do." But we walked along Swann's Way and all those places. They've got a little park--very badly kept--in honor of Proust.

It was all very interesting, and all the things he writes about are there in that little house. [Proust] described [in *A la Recherche du temps perdu*) what he called his grandmother's house; it was not his grandmother's house; it was an aunt's house. I got the impression [from the novel] that the garden was a great place--you remember how she used to go out and walk, even in the rain, up and down IS in the garden--and the garden is infinitesimal. It's just a little bit in front of the house, and she just walked up and down there.

The gate was still there, and the bell still rings that they always listened for when Swann was coming.

1974, France, Spain: We started in Rocamadour in France and followed the Knights Templar's journey to Santiago de Compostela, and that was great fun. We followed that route and then went back all along the northern coast back into France and back to Paris. The two also made several trips to Scotland, the Highlands, the Orkneys, Skye, and the Outer Hebrides, the last of which Jessie characterized as "just delightful." Ben particularly enjoyed it, according to Jessie, "because he got to see a great many standing stones."

As it happened, Ben and Jessie were often traveling together on her birthday, with some happy consequences for her.

I had some very memorable birthday dinners. One of them was at La Pyramide, which I don't think is a three-star any more, but it was. The French used to say that it was the best restaurant in France and therefore the best restaurant in the world. It was a marvelous place; it's a small restaurant out in the country, and nowhere but in France would people go those distances to eat in a restaurant, but we did.

Another one of my birthday dinners was at Tour d'Argent, the one restaurant that I think is worth going to just for the decor--and usually I don't feel that way. You know where it is--on the Left Bank and that rounded front looks on the Seine and on Notre Dame de Paris. Ben had a table that was right in the front and overlooked all this. The ceiling is not a mirror, but it's something like a dark mirror, and you see the bateaux mouches sailing upside down across the ceiling in the reflection. It's just marvelous. The meal was excellent, of course, too, but the decor was just as excellent.

They didn't have to eat in three-star restaurants to eat well, however. Particularly in France, it was always possible to find good food, even in the most out-of-the-way places. Once they stopped for lunch in the provinces at a small restaurant that was housed in a mill, and Jessie had a lobster bisque which she pronounced "absolutely perfect." They had found the place in the Michelin Guide, without which Ben never traveled in France. He told us on one of our trips that there seemed to him to be so many conflicting ideas in the Bible that he could never understand what someone meant by professing to believe in it. In perhaps the most concise revelation possible of what belief meant to him, he then declared, "Now, I believe in the Michelin Guide." The pictures, such as the following vignettes, that Jessie has drawn of their being together on these trips must recall to those who ever traveled with Ben memories rich with the comfortable atmosphere, the congeniality, the humor, and the endless fun that were among the great rewards of spending time with him.

> One summer when we went from England to France, we went through those hills in France where all the wild thyme grows and the wild lavender, and there's lavender honey for sale all along the way. We just had a ball. He (a friend who had joined them for part of the trip, as some friend or another sometimes did] and Ben knew every musical comedy song that ever had been written, I think. They sang those things--particularly Gilbert and Sullivan; both of them knew all the words and all the tunes--and they sang at the top of their lungs. We all had a hilarious time--and topped it off with that dinner at La Pyramide.

Whether Ben traveled with a companion or alone, he always took a good many books with him, some that he was reading for his research or for courses, others that he just wanted to read. Knowing his habits, people often gave him books--especially ones which they liked and wished Ben to read--when he was preparing to leave. Perry Dillon, for instance, gave Ben the boxed set of Durrell's *The Alexandria Quartet* before Ben took off in the summer of 1961. Some weeks later Perry received a postcard: "Thanks for the books. I enjoyed reading them on my way to Egypt. Alexandria is not like it was portrayed in the book. Ben."

When he flew, he always read, and since he took hundreds of flights all over the world in his lifetime (always first class because of his size), it follows that of the countless volumes he read over the years, a great many were read on airplanes. As is the case with most avid readers, certain sizes and formats of books especially appealed to Ben, particularly when it came to books that he took with him on trips. He found the Pleiade editions of the great French publishing house, Gallimard, to be precisely suited for reading on planes; the books are a very handy size, and, although compact, have quite readable print. He had read in its entirety, in French, *La Comedie Humaine* of Balzac, printed by Gallimard in ten Pleiade edition volumes, and most of it he read on airplanes.

It was Ben's custom to note on the fly-leaf of each of his books where and when he bought it. The history of his purchase of the complete ten-volume set of *La Comedie Humaine* is a telling one. The first volume that he bought was Volume V in Paris on September 4, 1957, probably to be read on the flight back to the States after his late summer trip to Yugoslavia.

It was on that visit to Yugoslavia that he found himself stranded in a small town one night when the bus he was on broke down. No hotel accommodations were available, but someone told him there was a quite comfortable whorehouse that would put him up for the night. Ben demurred. Wasn't there anything else, he wanted to know. Well, yes, there was a monastery a few kilometers out of town, and the monks there would sometimes take in overnight lodgers. Ben had someone drive him there. The monks spoke no English [or French, or German) and Serbo-Croatian was a language Ben did not know at all. When he told this story, we asked him how he managed to arrange for the room with them. "Oh, we did that in Latin," he said.

Volumes II and VI of *La Comedie Humaine* were ordered from Paris in March 1958, the spring before his first extensive trip to Africa. He bought Volumes III and IV in New York on December 30, 1958, Volume I in Athens on August 31, 1959, and Volumes VII, VIII, IX, and X, completing the set, in New York on December 28, 1959. He probably read the last four volumes the following summer on one of his most fascinating voyages: a cruise to the South Pacific.

It was no ordinary cruise. Ben embarked from San Francisco at 2:30p.m., Friday, June 10, 1960, on a sailing vessel bound for the Marquesas and Tahiti, following the path of a journey that Melville had made. The passengers shared various duties with the regular crew, and everyone was obliged to do so. Ben was advised to bring deck shoes and a pith helmet, but he could be obstinate and was on this occasion, insisting that the shoes he had would do very well and that he didn't need a helmet either. His sister, Betty, who was with him in San Francisco the day he sailed, said that as soon as Ben got on board, he realized his error regarding the shoes and was able to return to shore long enough to buy the first pair of tennis shoes he had ever owned; they were very likely the last pair he ever owned as well. He did not, however, give in on the pith helmet and later admitted that he had been wrong about that, too; the South Pacific sun proved to be punishing. Luckily, he was able to borrow one from someone else on board.

He charted the seven-and-a-half week voyage on a huge nautical map of the Pacific, placing an X and the date at their daily position, along with notations for the following dates:

June 19: 1054 miles from San Francisco; average 4.9 knots per day
June 21: 138 miles, 5.5 kts. average - 25 hours
June 24 and 25: doldrums
June 30 [at the equator]: 181 miles@ 7.5 knots
July 4: sighted Ua Huka at 5:50 a.m. anchored Taio Hae Bay midnight
July 5: Taio Hae
July 6: to north side of island, Atiheu Bay
July 7: 0100 left Atiheu, 0700 arr Taio Hae, left 1330, arr Hua Pou 1900
July 8: 1230 left Hua Pou
July 11: 9:20 p.m. sighted Takaroa
July 12: 0900 ashore; sailed 1630
July 15: arr Papeete 0600
July 21: left Papeete 1130, arr Moorea 1500
July 25: left Moorea 1530
July 26: arr Bora Bora 1700
July 29: 0700 lv. Bora Bora; 1600 arr Raiatea (Uturoa)
July 30: 0930 left Uturoa, 1145 arr Opoa, 1600 left Opoa
Aug 1: arr Tahiti (Punaauia)

On the page following the nautical map in the scrapbook is a map of Ua Huka drawn in Ben's hand; the names of various coves and bays are written in as well as the names of several native tribes in the areas of the island which they inhabit. He was a quite good cartographer and urged his students to be; for some years, on the weekly reading quiz in the first half of the British literature survey course, he required the students to draw an outline that was recognizably Great Britain and locate on it some two dozen places.

The familiar heavy tracing on road maps of Tahiti and Moorea indicate that he drove completely around those islands along the coast roads. From Tahiti he flew to Suva in the Fiji Islands and, after exploring the island of Viti Levu, took another boat, the Aoniu, on August 11, sailing to the Vava'u, Tongatabu, and Tonga Islands and then back to Fiji, whence he flew to Auckland on the north island of New Zealand and drove around over the northern half of the island, going as far south as Lake Taupo. He returned to Auckland and flew to Sydney.

In Australia, he took planes to the places he wanted to visit, and then rented cars to explore the immediate environs. The cities he has marked on the road map are Sydney; Melbourne, Adelaide, Brisbane, cairns, and Alice Springs. Most of them, including Alice Springs, have the roads in areas up to fifty miles around them marked.

His next stop, early in September, was the Samoa Islands, where he drove around the islands of Tutuila in American Samoa and Upolu in Western Samoa. From there he flew to the Hawaiian Islands, touring Oahu and Hawaii before returning home.

On the list reproduced at the beginning of this chapter, the foregoing trip, which lasted over three months, appears very simply as "Australia, New Zealand, Hawaii, Tahiti, South Seas." The scrapbooks show that every place mentioned on the list represents the same kind of thorough investigation of an area, a country, or, in some instances, a continent, as the South Seas venture. To regard Ben's maps carefully staggers the imagination; it is difficult to comprehend how anyone could have gone so many places, seen so much of the planet, observed first-hand so many wonders, and experienced so many different cultures in so brief a space as one lifetime. As I worked through the scrapbooks, I made notes from the maps on each page. I have reproduced below the notes from pages 83 through 92 of the first book, pages which chronicle the 1958 voyage to the Belgian Congo, South and East Africa, Egypt, Jordan, and Israel.

The page number is followed by the kind of map or kinds of maps on the page. The place names are departure, stopover, and destination points for flights (I was often unable to determine the direction of travel, so the order does not necessarily indicate which is which) and places along a marked route where Ben drew heavy dots to represent his having spent some time there; or, occasionally, when several routes from one point to another are possible, I have named some interim towns to indicate the route marked on the map. Words appearing in all capital letters are those written in Ben's hand on the maps.

83   Sabena Airline: from Western Europe to Tripoli - Stanleyville; Kano –
      Leopoldville West African Airways: Roberts Field - Abidjan – Accra
      Air France: Paris - Dakar; Dakar - Ouagadougou; Lagos - Brazzaville;
      Paris - Rome - Naples; Marseilles - Ajaccio; Paris – Madrid Republic of

Liberia: Monrovia - Klay - Born Hill; Monrovia - loop through Harbel and Roberts Field

84 Belgian Congo: Congo t rip--on the river from Stanleyville - Isangi - Coquilhatville - Leopoldville; from Leopoldville s. through Madimba to just northeast of Thysville; in east - loop from Uganda n. of Lac Eduoard - Margherita Peak - Beni - Lubero - s. end of lake - Goma - Kesenyi (n. end of Lac Kivu) – Ruhengeri - Kisolo (Uganda)

85 Nigeria: Lagos and about 10 miles n. UAT aeromaritime: Paris - Marseilles - NIAMEY – OUAGADOUGOU; Brazzaville – Livingstone French Equatorial Africa & Cameroon: Brazzaville - Leopoldville

86 Ghana: Accra - e. on coast to Terna and Chemu Lagoon; Accra - Aburi; Accra - loop through Achimota

87 South African Airways: Johannesburg - Windhoek; Johannesburg - Francistown; Johannesburg - Bulawayo; Johannesburg – Salisbury Rhodesia-Nyasaland: Livingstone - Victoria Falls canadair: Salisbury - Dar es Salaam Central African Airways: Livingstone - Bulawayo

88 10-in-1 maps of southern Africa: Cape Town - loop to Cape of Good Hope; Cape Town e. to Mossel Bay - n. to cango Caves - s. to George - Plettenberg Bay – Port Elizabeth - Grahamstown - King Williams Town – East London - Umtata - Kokstad - Pietermaritzburg – Durban - Stanger (loop Kranskop) - Empangen - Hluhluwe (into Umfolozi Game Reserve·) - Lourenco Marques – Kruger Game Preserve (almost every road south of Malopene Rest Camp in the Park is marked); Cape Town Laingsburg - Beaufort West - Britstown - Kimberly - Bloemfontein - Maseru - Bethlehem (loop Kestell - Fouriesburg) - Frankfort - Johannesburg - Pretoria; Johannesburg - Bethel - Chrissiesmeer - Lochiel - Mbabane (off-road loop) - Bremersdorp – Stegi (off-road loop) - Goba - Lourenco Marques; Johannesburg - Witbank - Nelspruit - into Kruger Preserve to Tshokwane; Pretoria - Middelburg - Lydenburg - Sabi - Graskop - into Kruger Preserve to MALA MALA; Windhoek - Etosha Game Park - along south shore of Etosha Pan - HALPLI[?] – Okaukuejo EAA airline: Nairobi - Mombasa - Tanga - Zanzibar – Dar es Salaam - Blantyre

89 Egypt: Alexandria - Tanta - Benha - Cairo; Cairo - s. along and either side of Nile - Luxor - Aswan and continuing along the Nile south off

the map; Cairo sw across Western desert to Birket Qarun; Cairo - e. across Eastern desert to Suez, continuing east off the map Uganda-Kenya-Tanganyika: from Belgian Congo e. to Kisoro - Masaka - Kampala (Lake Victoria) - Mumias (spur s. to Kisumu on the equator) - Eldoret - Sergoit - Kaptagat - Londiani (spur sw to Kericho) – Nakuru (loop Thompsons Falls - Nyeri TREETOPS - Fort Hall - Nairobi - Gilgil) - Nairobi; Nairobi - Narok - MASAI MARA RESERVE – KEEKEROK LOBO WILDLIFE LODGE - SERONERA – Lion Kijabe (loop - SERENGETI - Hill - Ngorongoro crater (spur to center] - Maku yuni – Arusha - Namane - Lake Amboseli - Emali) - Nairobi; Nairobi - Athi River (loop Arusha - Moshi - (spur Marangu (Kilimanjaro)] - Teveta- Mtito Andei- EmaliNairobi

90   Unidentified airline: Cairo - Port Sudan - Asmara - Addis Ababa – Nairobi Ethiopia: Gondar - Azazo; Gondar - Dabat; Bahr Dar on south point of Lake Tana to and several miles along the Abbai (Blue Nile); Addis Ababa- Mojjo- Nazareth - Awash – Metahara

91   Jordan: Jerusalem s. to Bethlehem - Hebron; Jerusalem - n. to Nablus; Jerusalem - e. to Jericho - north shore of Dead Sea - Amman; Jericho - Salt - Amman; Amman s. to Tafila - Petra; Amman n. to Jarash Ramtha into Syria Lebanon: Beyrouth n. along coast to Jbail; Beyrouth - Baabda - Chtaura - Ravak - Baalbek; Chtaura - Masnaa - Damascus; Ravak - Bar Elias

92   Israel: Tel Aviv - Jerusalem; Tel Aviv - Rishon le-Zion (loop) - Ashqelon - Sa'ad - Beersheba - Beit Qama - Rishon le-Zion; Tel Aviv - Hadera (loop) - Tiberius - along coast of Lake Tiberius to Mount of Beatitudes - Nazareth - Haifa - Mount Carmel - Hadera - Tel Aviv El Al airline: Tel Aviv - London - New York

Some time in the 1950s Ben discovered the joys of photography, which he had previously eschewed largely because of his distaste for that sort of tourist for whom the only point of going somewhere is to take a picture of it--and then, perhaps, to bore friends with the results. He described the type as someone who rushes up to the front of Notre Dame de Paris, takes a picture, and rushes off, never appreciating anything about the cathedral or even seeing it in any meaningful sense of the word. I don't know if he feared that carrying a camera would actually turn him into one of these odious creatures or if he simply did not want to be mistaken for one. Whatever his reservations about it, he overcame them. He began with prints, but in a few years the problems of storage became apparent, and he changed over almost entirely to slides. He had thousands of them and never, to my knowledge, showed them unless he were asked.

He rarely took pictures of people, and almost never people he knew; I do remember vividly a picture of a gnarled, sunburnt herdsman, very colorfully dressed, sitting in front of his tent that Ben took somewhere in Mongolia, but normally he tried to avoid having people in his pictures. When questioned about it, he said he had no trouble remembering what his friends look like, so he didn't need photographs of them and that there were very few reasons ever to take pictures of people he didn't know. He particularly liked natural scenes, especially mountains, and loved to photograph flowers and wildlife. He had one slide from his summer in South America of a tapir that did not, strictly speaking, qualify as wildlife; it was the pet of a family of missionaries living in the jungles of Ecuador with whom he had spent several days. When he showed the slide, he commented that the tapir was altogether tame and quite agreeable and that he had petted it.

For a good part of his life, Ben had it in mind to visit every country in the world, and he came very close to his goal; before the extensive changes in the African political boundaries were made, Ben said, he had been to all but twenty-six countries. One of those was China, which he desperately wanted to see. When China began opening up a little, among the first people to be allowed into the country were ping-pong players. We knew how he longed to be able to go and teased him about learning to play ping-pong so he could. If nothing else had been possible, I think he might have. He tried to get in with every tour he found out about for years. One year a group of farmers was being allowed in, and Ben applied to go with them, but was denied. Fortunately, the thawing of China's relations with the West continued, and in the summer of 1975 he went with a group of about twenty-five, most of them business people. Here is their itinerary; once again, what appears in all caps is written on the itinerary in Ben's hand:

Sept.   1 (M)   Arr. Peking at 15:00   BEIJING HOTEL
        2 (T) in Peking   MONGOLIAN REST.
        3 (W) DISTINGUISHED GUEST REST.
        4 (T) "
        5 (F) "
        6 (S) "
        7 (S) Dep. Peking at 9:10 by Air,
                arr GUOJI HOTEL
                Shanghai at 10:50 SIEHNAN REST.
        8 (M)   in Shanghai

9 (T) "	
10 (W)	"
11 (T)"	
12 (F)	Dep. Shanghai at 7:45 by Air, arr. Changsha at 9:05
13 (S)	Dep. Changsha at 12:50 by Air, arr. Kweilin at 14:05
15 (M)	in Kweilin
16 (T)	Dep. Kweilin at 13:45 by Air, arr. Kwangchow at 15:05
17 (W	in Kwangchow DONGFONG HOTEL
18 (T)	" PANHSI REST.
19 (F)	Exit [to Hong Kong] at 8:20 by Train via Shumchun

On the first of his postcards to us from China he wrote "This is one trip that does live up to expectations! We had 6 days in Peking & hated to leave it." And shortly after his return we had the following report:

> . . . I escaped from Chairman Saunders, who prepares his chickens differently--chops them into bite-sized chunks, replete with unidentifiable bones--the only drawback to Chinese cooking, which otherwise ranged from good to firstrate. Otherwise also the trip was a complete success. We saw as much as possible in 19 days, nicely mixed--palaces & communes & scenery &.factories & schools & Great Walls--no, only one of those. The Ch'in Emperor's tomb, however, is several hundred miles west of where we were.

China was the last "new" country he went to; in his scrapbooks, the map of China is the final map. His later voyages are traced on the maps from earlier times. In a sense, the China trip was the great traveler's last adventure, crowning an astonishing career. In 1979 or 1980, his home was burglarized twice; in the first, some of the silver that had been his mother's was taken. The second burglary followed shortly thereafter; the burglars apparently came back for the rest of the silver, and they also took Ben's very expensive camera. Ben was somewhat distressed by the loss of the silver, not because of its monetary value, but because it had belonged to his mother. The loss of the camera bothered him not at all. He told me that he'd been everywhere he wanted to go except for places he wanted to see again, "and I already have pictures of them," he said.

Ben had always been able to make his peace with whatever limitations came his way; that was perhaps his greatest virtue. Being content with where he was, wherever he was, made up a not inconsiderable portion of what enabled him to live the closest thing possible to a completely happy life. When his car broke down in Fort Stockton, Texas--twice--he sat in the showroom of the Buick dealership and peacefully read his books, only casting an occasional glance at the new, ostensibly functional Buicks. He accepted the end of his great odyssey with the same equanimity. In the fall of 1980, he wrote the following:

Dear J[ohn] & S[usan]--
　　I have spent two hours in the port of Valona, Albania, in 1939. Both reasons you name have influenced my increasingly stay-at-home state, but the main reasons are
1) I am busy
2) I grow old
3) I don't really want to see Equatorial Guinea.
　　I'll be on off-campus duty in spring, probably in N. Eng. What about Cape Cod?
. . . You don't seem to be getting to F'v. I have a counterproposal, but I drive a hard bargain. Since I've paid both my income tax & my Am. Express bill, I'd like to give a party in honor of my becoming a senior citizen--say in L. R. on Nov. 1 (Sat. before my apotheosis, but date not nonnegotiable), on condition that:

　　1) You induce Jack [Butler] to let me buy him a Skyways ticket--I do not want to drive.

　　2) You & Susan & Jack not bicker about letting me pay the hotel bill at the Sheraton.

　　3) You meet me at the airport & drive us to a bar that serves Margueritas (I'm pretty sure the Sheraton would fit that bill) & return me to the airport late Sunday morning.

　　4) You agree to have dinner at Jacques & Suzanne's & not fight the waiters.

Notice his spelling of Margarita; his French was ever so much better than his Spanish.

We had the party. The bar was Johnny Wink's famous traveling bar, described below. Ben and I split a rack of lamb at Jacques & Suzanne's; nobody fought the waiters. We all stayed up late and had a fine breakfast together on Sunday morning. Ben was not in Equatorial Guinea; he was, as he almost always was, just exactly where he wanted to be.

CHAPTER SIX

"He was an authentic genius, certainly the most widely read man and the person with the most retentive memory I have ever known."

> — Richard Marius, Director of Expository Writing, Harvard University; member of the Woodrow Wilson Foundation Fellowship selection committee, 1965-1972

"He was a man who seemingly had read everything and could recall it verbatim."

> — Claude Gibson, graduate student and staff, Department of English, University of Arkansas, Fayetteville, 1960-1976

"I really and truly believe that he knew more in breadth and depth about world literature than anybody else living. I have no doubt that you could have gone in and said, 'I'd like to have a little summary of Persian literature' and pick out any period, and he could have given a thirty-minute lecture on it—dates, authors, books. Come in the next day and ask the same thing about Canadian authors, and he could have done that, too."

> — Claude Faulkner, Chairman, Department of English, University of Arkansas, Fayetteville, 1948-1971

"I recall three renaissance men in my entire life who had this sweep of interests and knowledge—what I call a renaissance idealism; they were all different in their ways, but they had that sweep—none quite as broad and deep as Ben's."

> — Leo Van Scyoc, Professor, Department of English, University of Arkansas, Fayetteville, 1957 to present

"It was at these (Woodrow Wilson Foundation Fellowship] interviews that Ben demonstrated his tremendous store of knowledge. It was not that he went out of his way to show it; it was just that he had something to contribute no matter what the subject. A renaissance man. I have known only two other people with nearly his breadth of

\em is [Richard] Marius. Though we all asked questions of the ̲...̲u̲i̲d̲a̲t̲e̲s̲, one of us would lead, and so Ben had the literature and English candidates. His usual procedure was to ask for some book the candidate wanted to talk about. He always knew more about it than the candidate. His own reading was of course penetrating. Some of the books were to me at least pretty obscure. And it seemed to make little difference as to the language of the work. Ben had usually read it in the original."

> — Lyell Behr, Professor of Chemistry and Dean of Arts and Sciences, retired, Mississippi State University, member of the Woodrow Wilson Foundation Fellowship selection committee, 1963-1972

The foregoing comments are typical of reminiscences of Ben in that they cite one of the most frequently mentioned aspects of Ben's character: his vast knowledge. As astounding as Ben Kimpel's voyages about the world may have been, his most extensive travel was unquestionably in "the realms of gold."

His personal library was contained in hundreds of feet of book shelves both in his home and at his office and consisted of thousands of volumes, ranging from reproductions of early Sanskrit texts and the Egyptian Book of the Dead to contemporary writers from all over the world. Built-in bookcases, filled with books from the floor or cabinets to the very high ceiling, covered two of the walls in the large, split-level living room which accounted for well over half the total floor space in his home. It is not unusual to see a great many books in the home of an English teacher, but it may be more unusual for that teacher to have read every book on display. Ben had. As another instance of his sense of honor and integrity, he would not put a book on his book shelves until he had read it; he kept any books that he bought or that had been given to him in one of the cabinets beneath the shelving in the lower part of the room until he had read them.

Almost all of the volumes displayed in the living area were primary texts; he rarely purchased books of criticism unless they were classics, relying rather on library copies for his extensive reading in secondary texts. Novels, books of poetry, and dramatic works from the world over in a dozen languages were organized in what many considered a peculiar way: they were arranged chronologically according to the birth dates of the authors, anonymous works according to the dates they were written or published. The works of a given author were likewise put in the order of their composition or publication. Another proof of Ben's exceptional memory was that he could go directly, without the least hesitation, to any title whatsoever in his vast collection.

Most of the books displayed in the main room of his home were works of literature, although a large number of history and philosophy books were also found there. Other texts, including those on such wide-ranging subjects as biology, physics, chemistry, and mathematics, he kept elsewhere--some were on shelves in one of his closets, as I recall, and others, although he had read them, were kept in the cabinets which served as the temporary quarters for unread books.

Once I knew about his policy of putting his books on the shelves only after he had read them, every time I entered his house I was overwhelmed anew at the sight of his library. He was not an especially fast reader; in fact, he admitted to being really quite slow. One reason for this lack of speed, however, was that he habitually took copious notes on anything he was reading for the first time and often made additional notes on subsequent readings. Virtually every book he owned had either notes on the front and back fly-leaves or loose pages of notes stuck into them or, not unfrequently, both. His notes never fail to bring to my mind the miserly Plewshkin in Gogol's *Dead Souls*: every square centimeter of a page is filled with Ben's already cramped hand reduced to half its usual size. His notes for the Pound book are also small and crowded on the pages, a fact which multiplied first Duncan Eaves' and then David Strain's difficulties with trying to carry the work forward after Ben's death.

Like smoking, reading was both a pleasure and a habit for Ben. He read to learn, he read to relax, but above all he read because he loved to read; he made up for his lack of speed with consistency. As he mentioned in one of the letters to Duncan from Italy, he had much time after the libraries closed at one "mainly to read and eat." Practically every moment he ever spent on airplanes—thousands of hours—he spent reading. It was his habit to read for a time in the morning before going to school, and he relaxed an hour or two upon returning home in the afternoon by reading, usually before reading something else after dinner for some other purpose—his research, for example. He also generally read for pleasure just before retiring. Add to this time all the hours he must have spent in train stations, airports, waiting rooms of various sorts—you can be sure that he was reading. And his retention was phenomenal.

One of the courses Ben offered was a one-semester study of John Milton, whom Ben admired for many reasons, not the least of which was his extensive reading in many different languages. Ben used to say that, because of his energies on the one hand and the subsequent proliferation of printed books on the other, Milton may well have been the last person in the history of the world who had read everything that was available to be read in his time. I imagined a touch of envy along with the immense admiration in his voice when he said this--not that Ben wanted to read everything available in print by any means, only everything worth reading, but even that was no longer possible. He was forced to be selective; however, for most people the idea of selectivity becomes almost meaningless in light of the thousands and thousands of books Ben had read. But, as Leo Van Scyoc pointed out, Ben "was impatient with certain types of literature; he'd give things a try, though. He'd read to be sure he was speaking from an informed position."

Ben said of himself, "I have never forgotten anything I wanted to remember." What he wanted to remember included everything from show tunes to Shakespeare; from geography, dates, facts, and names to ideas and attitudes; from the profound to the trivial. Leo Van Scyoc has said that, although as far as he knew Ben never taught Shakespeare, "good land, he could quote it—and not just the standard speeches. There's no question in my mind that he made a part of himself everything he read." Claude Gibson has recalled that "over the din of 'arena registration' those working the tables would yell out all kinds of challenges to Kimpel trying to stump him on some obscure piece of information. No one ever succeeded in my memory. And I have seen students at a party call out the names of poems, which he would dutifully proceed to recite from memory."

Most people who knew Ben were fascinated by his remarkable powers of recall. Those powers contributed much to his success as a student of languages, as a teacher, as a scholar, as a brilliant conversationalist, as a delightful companion, and as a player of games. The following anecdotes, like Jessie O'Kelly's, quoted previously, concern his memory for music.

> . . . There used to be a thing called the Dallas Opera Festival which consisted of galas two or three times a year. I don't think Ben missed a one, and he would go to these things even at considerable inconvenience. I had in those days a piebald grey Volkswagen beetle, and four of us went [David and Emily Hart, Robert Morris, and Ben]. In a gesture of great gallantry, Ben and Robert insisted that Emily should ride in the passenger's seat in the front; so we drove from Fayetteville to Dallas with Ben and Robert in the back seat, and, of course, we had luggage for four people: it was a snug fit. But we drove down to Dallas, saw a lot of opera, and everybody had a good time. There was a Sunday matinee that time, and we all had early Monday morning classes, so it was decided that we would see the Sunday matinee and then leave Dallas about sunset and drive through the night back to Fayetteville.
>
> A lot of the road was torn up and there were lots of delays, and the trip took much longer than usual—at least ten hours. Well, by the time dark had fallen, it was clear that we were going to be delayed, and spirits were tending to sag—measurably and discernibly. Robert and Ben were once again

wedged into the back seat. Ben proposed that we should while away the time by singing. There were not too many sorts of songs that all four of us knew together; we went through a brief phase of "Row, Row, Row Your Boat" and "Frere Jacques," but those don't take you very far. We all knew some of the lyrics to some of the Gilbert and Sullivan Savoy operas, so we started with those. I think that *Yeoman of the Guard* and *Pirates of Penzance* were probably the first ones because I, at least, know fragments of some of the lyrics of some of the songs from those two more than the others, and that's the way it was—except that Ben knew them all. In the end, he sang—sometimes with intermittent accompaniment from the rest of us—he sang all of the songs to all of the Savoy operas. We were in the dark vastnesses of Oklahoma by then, but not all that close to Fayetteville; so then he started in on the light operettas of the 1920s and thirties—Rudolf Friml and people like that. "Blue Moon"—"No, No, Nanette"—he knew them all. And he was still singing when we came in to Fayetteville from the west as the sun was coming in from the east the next morning. We were on the road at least ten hours; I think that he must have been singing eight of those hours. He never repeated himself; he still had operettas to go. He knew them all.

Professor Hart's story also underlines both Ben's passion for grand opera and his unflagging good nature. If there were good opera to be seen in Dallas, Memphis, or Tulsa, Ben would be sure to go, and attending the opera was one of his customary activities in his travels to New York and abroad. He also owned many, many recordings to which he regularly listened on his very fine stereo system with its huge Klipsch speakers. His nephew, Bill Warner, who lived with Ben for a year while Bill was still in high school, complained to his mother that he sometimes found it difficult to study because Ben played his music so loud, particularly the operas. As part of his routine, Ben would vacuum his house on Saturday morning, and he generally put an opera on the stereo and turned the volume up so that he could hear the music over the sound of the vacuum cleaner. If Wagner booming out over the drone of a vacuum cleaner did not wake the Confederate dead in the cemetery across the street from his house, I fear Gabriel's horn has little chance of doing the job.

I have heard Ben sing portions of arias in Italian, German, and French; I do not doubt that he knew entire operas, very likely including the recitativi. Four of his five favorite operas were composed by his favorite composer in general, Mozart: The *Marriage of*

Figaro, The Magic Flute, Don Giovanni, and *Cosi fan tutte;* the fifth was Moussorgsky's *Boris Godunov.*

The range of Ben's tastes suggested by his fondness for music as diverse as popular show tunes, the music of the Beatles (although, on the whole, contemporary rock music did not hold much appeal for him, he did like the Beatles], and opera was reflected in most other areas as well: literature, art, natural beauty, people, and food among them. When Johnny said to Ben on one occasion that he seemed to have loved a great many things in his life, Ben replied, "Well, I've loved whatever I *could* love." Yet he was not lacking in discrimination; he simply had the generosity of mind that seeks the best in whatever it encounters and the perspicacity to find it. Add to these qualities a Gargantuan capacity to appreciate or, to use one of his favorite phrases, "to get a kick out of" things, and it should be clear why being with him was such fun and why he seemed always to be enjoying himself, regardless of what he happened to be doing or where he happened to be.

His fondness for good food is another subject that often comes up in any discussion of Ben; the following anecdotes attest to his something more than legendary love of eating:

> ... My own introduction to Stilton was under Dr. Kimpel's tutelage. He took us to dinner one time on a memorable evening during the Christmas season at one of his favorite French restaurants in London's Soho when Nancy [Talburt] and I were there, and the Kernodles were there and Preston Macgruder. Nancy and I resolved to follow him step by step in what he considered an acceptable meal—the whole catastrophe, as Zorba said. The meal began just after the theater and continued until after one o'clock. I wish I could remember that whole menu. I know he started with Scotch, and when we were finally shown into the dining room he had a half a dozen oysters, and those were so good that he had half a dozen more. We had soup, and he may have had soup, too. But he went through everything from those oysters through the entree, and, of course, he ordered the very finest wine—he insisted that the wine was his treat—through dessert, through cheese. I can't recall everything, but I do remember the end: fresh strawberries and thick English cream in little silver bowls, and then the Stilton, and then the coffee. By that time it was past midnight, but he also wanted a liqueur, and Nancy and I were almost under the table; mercifully, my mind has blotted out much of the rest of the night and the next day. Nancy and I had to admit defeat; we didn't even think about food until around four o'clock the next day when we

were able to lift our heads for a cup of tea. The restaurant is now a pizza parlor.

Nothing gold can stay.

--Lyna Lee Montgomery

. . . Ben was always plagued by two conflicting desires: to be fashionably slim and to eat well. At one period he dieted under the inspiring slogan of 'Into the tux by Christmas!' Many years later, when he was teaching in Fayetteville and I was stationed in Bremen, we had lunch at Jacob's Weinrestaurant on the banks of the Elbe in Blankenese. Ben rationalized his choices from the menu by saying 'You can't get this in Arkansas,' acceptable enough when it came to such delicacies as smoked eel, but I challenged him on this claim when it came to a dessert of raspberries and cream. He was able to respond only inadequately to the effect that it was hard to get anyone to pick the berries any more. A good sign, I thought, of improving times and better jobs. Anyway, the raspberries and the thick cream (which you can't get anywhere in the States) were as good as they looked.

--Brynhild Rowberg

. . . When the interviews were over, we had dinner. Our payment was only $100 each year, which was pretty low; we must have averaged 100 hours apiece. I believe it was Ray Poggenburg who evolved the idea that we should eat well. And we did. In Cincinnati we had dinner at the Maisonette, in Memphis at Justine's, in New Orleans at Commander's Palace and Antoine's. We found out later that we spent the second largest amount on food of any of the committees, the highest being based in New York. As I am sure you know, Ben was a gourmet, and what might be called a 'good eater.' He knew of restaurants virtually every place in this country and in Europe as well. He had a fine knowledge of foods from everywhere as well as wines.

--Lyell Behr

For all his enthusiasm for fine food, however, I have never known anyone who relished a good cheeseburger more than Ben, and his favorite food in all the world was home-cooked southern fried chicken (conversely, his least favorite was franchised fried chicken). Lyell Behr added the following to his account of the scholarship committee's gastronomical extravagance:

. . . This is not to say that he (or we) always ate in upscale places. He could appreciate a good hamburger or barbeque. In Louisville he always had a hot brown sandwich for lunch at the Brown Hotel. It was an extensive concoction which as I remember contained turkey and ham and various salad vegetables. Brown gravy was poured over the assemblage.

On a postcard from Glacier National Park in July 1975, Ben wrote, "Having broadened my horizons with a buffalo cheeseburger in the Black Hills, I tried a Smoky Bear burger near the Little Big Horn & a Super Poppa Burger in Lewistown, Mont.—alas! the names of the latter were honorific, the meat was beef." When we first began traveling with Ben, that he would calmly order cheeseburgers using the often very silly names given them on menus amused us no end; but we got used to it as just another bit of evidence of how little he worried about appearances. Few people can escape from ego as thoroughly as Ben had. As one of his colleagues said, "I just don't think I could ever bring myself to say 'Super Pappa Burger' out loud in a public place."

Ben's spirits were never higher than when he was enjoying (or anticipating enjoying) a good meal, whether a cheeseburger or pheasant, and not many things could dampen his spirits like a bad one. We were lucky in our travels in the West; well over ninety percent of our meals were acceptable or better and some of them were really exceptionally good. Ben's wit and conversational genius seemed to be at their peak just before and during a good dinner. Watching Ben at a bad meal, however, had its interest. He was invariably optimistic when he sat down to eat, but when his hopes were dashed, course after course, his spirits often would sink a little lower with each new disappointment. Conversation would not be quite so lively, and sometimes he would even get a little testy; I've seen him all but pout during a disappointing meal.

As much as he enjoyed good food in fine restaurants, perhaps his keenest appreciation was for home cooking. He did some cooking himself, but aside from a few recipes—including one for a chocolate souffle that he had from his mother, apparently an excellent cook—he did not do much cooking. One thing he planned to do when he retired was learn to cook. Happily for him, two of his dearest friends, Jessie O'Kelly and Juliet Eaves, were both exceptionally good cooks, and he had, as it were, standing invitations from both of them. His students, some of whom were undoubtedly talented cooks and probably outdid themselves for Ben, also often invited him to dinner.

According to his calendars, Ben was asked to dinner at least once a week on the average. One of his most frequent hosts was Jessie O'Kelly, and not all of their meals together were arranged: "He was always appearing at the front door with his hands full of something," Jessie has reported, "either fine cheeses that he'd found somewhere or something. One time in the late afternoon he appeared; he had found fresh oysters and fresh shrimp. He had two bags of both, and I said, 'Why don't you come on in, and we'll cook the shrimp,' and he said, 'All right, but why don't we eat the oysters, too?' So we ate the oysters and the shrimp right there. It was such fun to do; I just loved it."

One famous story about his eating concerns a huge Esterhazy torte that Juliet Eaves had made for some occasion. Ben and Duncan were working on one of their projects at the Eaves home, and Juliet made it very clear to them before she retired that they were not to touch that torte. Well, they could not resist; first a little, thence to more, they sampled that delicious store and finished by eating the whole thing. Duncan wound up in the hospital. It never fazed Ben.

Ben's love of home cooking was reflected in a memorable disquisition delivered somewhere in Kansas as we drove eastward on our way back from the Colorado Rockies. Noon was approaching, stomachs were growling, and even small towns were scarce along our route. Ben, with small contributions from the rest of us, began describing what we were going to find in the next tiny dot on the map: Grandmother Parker's. Into the description of this idyllic place went every dish dear to Ben's heart. We would be seated at a long, family-style table, and soups, salads, homemade bread, real butter, heaping platters of fried chicken, gravy, homemade biscuits, good rich coffee, fresh fruit, real cream, and homemade pies of various sorts would be brought out to us, each in its turn, from the kitchen. Ben went into loving detail as he described each item on the menu, and the description went on for at least a quarter of an hour. Having finished with the last flaky crumb of the fresh apple pie, he sat in silence as we sped on through the wheat fields. Suddenly he exploded, "Damn it, why isn't there a Grandmother Parker's? It's not impossible to prepare food like that!"

Canned biscuits, corn starch pies, imitation anything, and franchised food of any sort were for Ben the worst kinds of abominations. Most of them he simply could not understand; "Nothing is easier to make than biscuits!" he would exclaim, genuinely puzzled about why anyone would ever use canned biscuits for anything. One of his wonderful parodies of modern advertising went this way: "A woman is in her kitchen, and Mrs. Olson comes in and says, 'I see you're still using real apples in your apple pie; no wonder your husband is leaving you!'" And in response to a former student's contention that America is superior to Europe, Ben had this to say:

> . . . I am completely convinced, knowing (as we all do) that the New World Symphony is much grander than Beethoven's 9th, that the Rockies are the tallest mountains in the world (is it four or five times as tall as the Alps?), that

the Mississippi makes the Amazon & Nile look like rivulets, & that American apple pie is the world's most natural & unspoiled dessert—no canned fruits such as the Italians use, no frozen pastry shells a la française, no filling eked out with corn starch, no additives & no substitutes, only the great, unspoiled Nature of America herself!

On one occasion, Johnny asked Ben, "If you could un-invent one thing in the twentieth century, what would it be?" Ben thought about it a good while, becoming a little agitated, then, shaking his jowls, said, "Well, in all conscience I'll have to say the atomic bomb, but if it weren't for that, I'd say Jello." "As close to *nothing* as anything can be," he pronounced it, which was also his judgment of most bread sold in the United States. In his Oxford lecture, Ben admitted, "I think maybe the real reason I love Pound is that he added cookery as an example of good craftsmanship. I'm constantly reminded of the fact that when he threw some of the army white bread out to the birds, they wouldn't eat it—and he thought they had very good taste."

In his tastes in beverages, Ben was also something of a purist. His preferred liquor was usually scotch, although if good Russian vodka were available, he would take it, and he also occasionally ordered a gin martini. He always drank margaritas before dinner in Santa Fe and Mexico, and he would drink an occasional daiquiri. He detested even the idea of frozen margaritas and daiquiris, however, and the rising popularity of various fruit daiquiris he viewed with both alarm and disgust. They simply weren't daiquiris as far as he was concerned; the only drink worthy of the name was made with real lime juice, rum, a little sugar, and nothing else, chilled and served straight up.

He generally preferred dry, full-bodied red wines. On a camping trip in Montgomery county in western Arkansas, he and Herman Sandford, Johnny Wink, Jack Butler, and perhaps some others, were unexpectedly joined one morning by another denizen of Arkadelphia, whose passions include the Arkansas wilderness and fine French wines. He had back-packed into the campsite on his way elsewhere in the wilds, and among his stores, sticking out from his pack, was a bottle—a Rothschild of good date. The resident campers invited him to stay for lunch with them, but, not wanting to intrude, he declined. Later in the morning, as the visitor sat talking with the others before moving on, Ben, who had not been present when he had been asked to stay, suggested to Herman that he extend an invitation. "I already have," Herman replied, "but he said that he'd better go on." Ben eyed the bottle in the visitor's backpack and said, "I think you ought to insist."

With his great capacities for food and drink, it should be noted that he stood in awe of the really great eaters in history. He once said that, although he believed the accounts to be factual, he simply could not comprehend how Balzac could consume the quantities of food and drink that he did. Even the meal in London described by Lyna Lee Montgomery pales in comparison to Balzac's recorded repasts. But Ben was nonetheless able to eat a great deal of food without feeling the least discomfort. His capacity for alcohol was also uncommonly great. I have seen him at the very most a little tipsy, and the quantities of liquor it took for him to arrive at that modest state were more than enough to put most people under the table.

If Ben ever wanted to be, in Miss Rowberg's phrase, "fashionably thin," you can be sure that the concern was his wanting to be able to eat whatever he wanted rather than any preoccupation with his appearance. It was his habit for years to diet during the months before a trip so he could eat as he pleased while traveling and still be able to get into his clothes. He hated to diet, but he had done so since he was a child and would dutifully eat his radishes and carrots in his office at noon and his tomato soup at night, consoling himself, no doubt, with visions of smoked eels and raspberries and cream. The following anecdote concerning one of Ben's diets was provided by Russ Goodyear:

> When he decided to go on the diet, Lyna Lee Montgomery, always helpful, suggested that he try the new liquid Seago. I happened to be in the office checking my mailbox and overheard a conversation that went something like this:
> "Those Seagos are great, Lyna Lee; I had two of them with my lunch."
> "No, no, Ben, you're supposed to have the Seago instead of lunch."

Most of the trips that we took with Ben, which usually occurred before one of his trips abroad, he began in pretty good shape. His pants were generally gathered beneath a cinched-up belt which would invariably be let out another notch or two before our trip ended but still with a little room for Europe left. Dieting became more difficult for him in the last few years of his life; "I've been dieting since I was a child," he is quoted as having said, "and I just can't bear to start another one." As a consequence, in the months before his death, he was as large as most of his friends could remember his ever having been. Few think that his weight had much if anything to do with his death, however. He had been heavy all his life, after all; his heart was certainly used to it, and when he had his cataract surgery only months before his death, the preliminary physical found his heart altogether healthy. According to his appointment book, he had been seeing a cardiologist regularly for years; he was no fool—he knew that his size and the way he lived could pose a real threat— but there is no indication that any danger signs whatsoever appeared at any time.

In a conversation with Lyna Lee Montgomery, bemoaning the losses that aging inevitably brings, Ben said, "God, won't it be awful when the stomach goes?" His sudden death at least spared him that. He was also spared having to endure in fact a cynical little fantasy he had: "After all these years of dieting, I'll be on my death-bed, and Duncan will rush in and say, 'Ben! They've come up with this tasteless, odorless, clear liquid that you can sprinkle on chocolate pie and it takes all the calories out!'" He could hardly think of a better aim for science and technology than that; it would have been in his view real progress.

Richard Marius has written a splendid account of his relationship with Ben. I began this chapter with a quotation from that account, and I could write no better conclusion than the one which the following excerpt from it provides.

> Airplanes were a large part of my life with Ben. I used to hate to fly, and at times I refused to get onto an airplane. Ben had a sense of resignation in life; what was to be would be. He never flinched before danger. One time we were flying home from a Woodrow Wilson committee meeting in Louisville. I had to take an Allegheny airlines flight (now US Air) from Louisville to Cincinnati and change planes to Knoxville. Cincinnati had (and probably still has) one of the most dangerous airports in the country, and a drenching rain was falling. On top of that Allegheny had lost two planes during the previous month. I was terrified. I told Ben, "I don't believe enough in God to pray to make a deal. But I do believe in you, Ben. What can I do to get back to Knoxville safely?" Ben had discovered that I had never read Proust. He said, "Promise to read all of Proust, and you will get safely home." I did, and I did. Alas, I got through only two of the three volumes in the Bibliothèque de la Pleiade and never completed—at least I have not yet completed the last. Even as I write I feel Ben's ghost reproaching me.
>
> . . . I met him in December 1965 in New Orleans. Raymond Paul Poggenburg, then head of the French department at Vanderbilt, had invited me to join the Woodrow Wilson Foundation Fellowship selection committee, and because the committee loved to eat well he put the first meeting in New Orleans. That was the meeting where we put our heads together over the some 400 dossiers we had collected from aspiring seniors in our region—Arkansas, Tennessee, Mississippi, and Kentucky—the Garden of God, I always called it. At that time we were trying to draw people into college teaching because there seemed to be a coming shortage. (Now people talk about such a shortage again, and like an old baseball player, I listen longingly for the umpire's call and the resurrection of a ghostly committee with a ghostly task.)

We met at the Charles Hotel on St. Charles Street—Ray, Earl Aliosi from the University of Louisville, Lyell Behr, who was then dean of liberal arts at Mississippi State, Ben, and me. I was by far the youngest of the group.

Ben was what he seemed always to be—large, redfaced, a little gruff, with coarse white hair, and a wonderfully genuine smile. I discovered that evening how much he enjoyed some of the sensual things of life—eating, drinking, and smoking. And good talk. I don't think I ever saw anyone enjoy talk as much as Ben did. I go back to that first evening together because Ben met me with a kind of examination. He wanted to know what I knew. It turned out that we both had a great talent for what some would call trivia—names and dates. At one point he asked me what some name meant to me. I do not at this moment recall what it was, but at the time I said, "I think he was a king in the Sandwich Islands in the nineteenth century." Either I knew what I was talking about or I hit on a lucky guess, for Ben nodded and exclaimed in the wheezing grunt of his that betokened as much admiration as he ever showed to anyone. From then on we were friends. Having chosen our short list of candidates in December, we interviewed our picks in Memphis, Nashville, and Louisville in January. These are towns that I still remember largely because of the restaurants—
Justine's in Memphis, Mario's in Nashville, the Old House in Louisville. Ben went through them all like fire through a barn.

I won't try to give you a chronology of the friendship except to say that in that year, 1965-6, I replaced someone temporarily on the committee and dropped off the following year. But the next year Ray Poggenburg asked to be relieved, and the Woodrow Wilson people in Princeton asked me to replace him as chair. Earl also stepped down. I appointed a friend of mine at the University of Tennessee, Ralph Norman, to take Earl's place, and we four made the committee from then until the Woodrow Wilson Fellowship program died away in 1972.

On becoming chairman I changed one thing: Ralph had taught at Miami University in Oxford, Ohio, and he knew how good Cincinnati restaurants were. We at first had our dossier reading meeting in December there instead of New Orleans. Then one January night in Louisville three of the four of us got food poisoning at the Old House. I think it was the snails. You will guess correctly that the one who escaped the malady was Ben. I got up that morning feeling wretched and completely nauseated. I skipped breakfast, but when we assembled in the interviewing room, I realized that I was about to vomit. All of us but Ben looked green. I excused myself and rushed to the elevator to go to my room. I threw up all over the elevator floor. Ralph and Lyell followed soon after, leaving a bemused Ben to interview that morning's candidates by himself while we recovered. We had perfect confidence in his choices.

From then on I changed the Louisville meeting to Cincinnati. We ate and we drank and we ate, and both Ben and Lyell smoked. Lyell smoked Pall Malls; Ben smoked Camels, one after another. I occasionally bummed a cigarette from one or the other, but I never was a confirmed smoker. Even then I knew that Ben smoked too much. Everyone who knew him saw him at one time or another reach for a new cigarette almost absent-mindedly while he puffed still on an old one. Yet he could out-drink and out-endure all the rest of us. In those days all of us drank a lot--far too much. Now I may drink a beer or a glass of wine, and once a month or so I have a drink of hard liquor. In those days we sloshed the stuff down like lemonade on a hot day.

We had our reasons. We interviewed kids sometimes fourteen hours a day, and at night we tore into food and drink as an escape from the steady concentration that, as you know, can be wearing. Sometimes I was ready to die from exhaustion. But Ben always plodded on, standing very straight as was his wont, always ready for another nightcap, always waiting for one of us to announce exhaustion and the resolution to go to sleep.

One night in Nashville we had to wait in the bar of a big restaurant for well over an hour for a table. It was the night Houston beat UCLA by two points for one of the rare defeats UCLA had when Lew Alcindor, who later changed his name to something else (I am no basketball fan), played. We watched the game, Ben without interest. He never had any interest that I could see in sports. The rest of us would watch just about anything. We watched, and we drank. We drank and drank and drank. By the time we got to our table, I hardly knew where I was. I ordered a prime rib, as did Ben. I dawdled over mine and then simply passed out on the table. I put my head down by my plate and passed out. My group let me sleep while Ben finished off his prime rib and ate mine, too. He was ready for a nightcap when we got back to the hotel.

When I became chairman, we started going back to one of the rooms at night and playing a word game called Botticelli. You probably know how it is played. Ben loved that game. Of course he was very good at it. It involved ingenious questioning and answering, a bit like the old game Twenty Questions, but much more imaginative. It always delighted me to see that big, formidable man lying back on a bed, smoking, his hard, rumpled trousers hiked up above his short socks, his face red with pleasure, playing that game as if it were at that moment the most important thing in the world.

He was amazing during interviews. He always began by asking a candidate in literature what he or she wanted to talk about. The candidate would ponder the question a moment and mention an author. Ben would ask, "What work?" The student would often look a little bewildered and come up sometimes with a title. Ben would then ask a specific question about a character, a scene. His memory was phenomenal. I recall that he was stumped only one time--when a student wanted to talk about Saul Bellow's Herzog. Ben said, "I have not read it." I thought the sky must fall. But the next time anybody mentioned Herzog, as someone did in a year or two, Ben was ready with the same amazing powers of recall that he showed for everything else in the literature of all the world.

He could not have done what he did without a splendid mind, but he also worked hard at remembering. At the MLA in San Francisco in 1979 we spent a lot of time together. Once I went up to his room to have a nightcap, and I found him—not unexpectedly—reading. I looked at the book and saw that he had pencilled in all sorts of comments in the front and the back. He could, I surmise, pick up any book he owned and see his own notes and recall something about it. It is a technique I have long used, and I was rather comforted to think that Ben did not remember everything spontaneously. I asked him once if he was a fast reader; he said, no, he was a very slow reader. But such things are relative. I always had the feeling that Ben had a special mind, one seldom seen. There can be no doubt that he was the best-read person I have ever known in my life. (At that same MLA we ended up waiting for planes in the San Francisco airport, and Ben ordered Irish coffee. I think we had five each. I passed out on the plane and woke up groggy and half sick back on the East coast. Ben, I am sure, got home to Fort Smith without thinking about a hangover.)

We had some hilarious moments. There was the busty cheerleader from Ole Miss who came in with claims of intellectual prowess that made her dossier glow. We brought her in for an interview, and the moment we saw her we knew that we had made a mistake. But Ben tried manfully. "What do you want to talk about?" he asked her. "Wahl, Ah jess love t'tawlk about Mister Fawlkner," she drawled. "Fine," Ben said. "Which one of the novels or short stories do you want to talk about?" She looked bewildered, astonished. "What?" she said. Ben patiently repeated his question. Now she looked utterly dismayed. "Wahl, Ah don' want to talk about jess one little bitty novel. Ah want t'talk about the whole thing." From then until the end of his life we would often say to each other at certain moments, "Ah don' want to talk about jess one little bitty novel. Ah want t' talk about the whole thing," and we would burst out laughing.

. . . I was married for the second time in 1970. Ben was in Cambridge, studying Chinese. I called him and told him I wanted him to come to my wedding in Mississippi. His presence would be my wedding gift. I sent him a ticket, and down he came to Memphis where my brother John met him and drove through hard rain to Greenville. It was my wife Lanier's first marriage, my second. I felt a strange reluctance to invite many of my old friends to a second marriage. The only ones I asked to come were the members of my Woodrow Wilson committee and my brother John. Ralph Norman was away, but Lyell and Ben were both there, and we had a delightful time. A cousin of Lanier's father gave us a big party the night before, a plantation house filled with crowds of people drinking champagne, and Ben circulated with benign aplomb through it all, quickly adored by all, comporting himself like a heavenly Buddha having the time of his life and making others feel that they were honored in his presence. We sat up late in a motel room later on, drinking with the pleasures of our years together. And on the morning of the wedding, March 21, we had a three-hour breakfast and a glorious time. I do not think I have ever seen anyone with Ben's sense of almost childish enjoyment of occasion.

At the church, Lanier's large clan sat on one side. My brother John was my best man, and Lyell was a groomsman. Only Ben and Lyell's wife, Pat, sat on my side of the church. When I walked out with the minister and saw Ben sitting there in his huge bulk, I thought, "It is enough."

CHAPTER SEVEN

"I don't hate football," Ben said, having been asked about his vehemence against the game; "I pray daily for its conversion." Into what, his interrogator wanted to know; Ben replied, "Oh, anything--bridge, croquet . . . ." He was the most down on football of any man I ever saw. As Lyell Behr has testified, Ben "expressed hope that Arkansas would lose all its games, and he had a pretty low opinion of people who wear hog snouts on the top of their heads." He was not reluctant to express his views on the subject, either, even though they represented, for many of his students, downright heresy. Indeed, that the game had come to be taken so seriously that such opinions would be considered heretical was the main reason he held them, for, as Mr. Behr has commented, "I don't believe he had anything against sports; it was what people did in the name of sports." One fall when Arkansas had beaten the University of Texas in their annual match and Ben learned of the outcome the next Monday in class, he groaned, "Oh, Lord, now that'll set up that damn Cotton Bowl pattern!"

The "Cotton Bowl pattern" that he had in mind entailed the prolongation to the Christmas holidays of the perpetual pep-rally mentality on campus that otherwise ended after the last regular season game, with people riding up and down in front of Old Main yelling and blaring their horns and students being hard-pressed to concentrate on much except the upcoming game. He taught many of his courses, while the English department was still housed in Old Main, in one of the classrooms at the front of the building, so that the noise was particularly distracting.

Johnny Wink and Jack Butler were wont to take on trips a football to throw around and, loving as they did to needle Ben, frequently attempted to force him into one of their impromptu roadside games. Ben was invariably fun to watch in these confrontations, which was, of course, their principal reason for being; he usually made some witty and withering remark about people who play football and generally acted the part of curmudgeon. However, one afternoon, much to our surprise, he breezily agreed to join in and positioned himself to take the snap from Johnny. As soon as the ball was in his hands, he straightened up, turned on his heel, took three deliberate steps, and thrust the ball into a trash can. He looked "pleased as punch," as he might have described it, and asked with mock innocence, "Isn't that what I was supposed to do with it?"

After Thanksgiving holidays, which he generally spent in Fort Smith at the home of his sister and her husband, who does like football, he would surprise his students by announcing the correct score of whatever professional game had been played on Thanksgiving Day. To be involved in whatever was going on was characteristic of him, and "When in Rome . . " He probably remembered more about the few games he saw than the most avid fans did.

He was a little more tolerant of baseball than of other sports, probably because enthusiasm for the game did not perceptibly intrude into other endeavors, such as trying to teach or to learn. But he also preferred baseball to football because in the game of baseball people do not deliberately try to hurt one another, at least not often. He had been to games as a child and had once seen Babe Ruth hit a homerun. But even in baseball his interest was minimal.

In the winter of 1982, Johnny and Jay Curlin went to Fayetteville for a week-end and joined David Strain and Ben for lunch at a local restaurant which ·had an enormous television screen covering one wall in the dining area. That day a basketball game between the Universities of Missouri and Oklahoma was being broadcast as the four sat down to eat. The following conversation attesting to Ben's great interest in the game ensued:

> "Who do you want to win, Ben?"
> "Who's playing?"
> "Missouri and Oklahoma."
> "Missouri."
> "Why?"
> "Well, because Missouri borders Arkansas."
> "So does Oklahoma."
> "I didn't say it didn't."

Such enthusiasm is rare, indeed. Ben summed up his attitude toward sports by telling an anecdote concerning the Shah of Iran, whose hosts, during a visit to England, were trying to persuade him to attend a horse race. The Shah declined. His hosts kept pressing him to go, and when he still declined, they asked him why. "I know that, in principle, one horse can run faster than another," the Shah responded, "and I'm not interested in the details."

Ben knew just enough about sports to get by when the occasion called for it. We visited him over a football week-end in Fayetteville, and he had gone to the grocery store some time after the game was over Saturday afternoon. As Ben was checking out, a pleasant young man who worked in the store asked him what he had thought of the game. Ben, of course, didn't even know who had played, much less who had won, and in fact only assumed he was referring to a football game because it was late September, but he liked this fellow and knew that it actually might hurt his feelings if Ben admitted not just his indifference but even his ignorance, so he said, "Well, I really think they should have punted on third down there in the fourth quarter." The young man, obviously impressed with Ben's sports acumen, heartily agreed.

In Missouri, some fifty miles from the Arkansas state line as we returned from one of our trips, Ben was stopped for speeding. The trooper made Ben go back and sit in the patrol car with him to talk. Johnny, Jack, and I became concerned as time passed and Ben was still being detained. Finally, he returned to the car, buckled himself in, and waved as the patrolman pulled out and left. Back on the road, we asked what had taken so long. "We were talking about football," he confessed. "He is very optimistic about Arkansas's chances next fall." We wanted to know what Ben had contributed to this discussion. "Oh, he did all the talking. When he first mentioned Arkansas football, I just nodded and said, 'Mm-hmm . . . Lou Holtz . . . .'"

Johnny, Jack, and I were all sports fans, a fact Ben pretended to be at a loss to understand, and we could always count on the subject to elicit Ben's wit. In answer to some mention of Larry Bird, a professional basketball player, Ben wrote in a letter discussing a future trip, "You'll tell me all about Larry Bird? Presumably not a pseudonym for Charlie Parker or a relative of Mrs. Lyndon Johnson?" He was also great fun on the subject of the names of teams, particularly those professional teams who had moved from one section of the country, where the name may have been appropriate, to another where it was not, such as the Minneapolis Lakers, now the Los Angeles Lakers, and the New Orleans Jazz, who became the Utah Jazz. Ben would screw up his nose at these revelations as if he had just bitten into a bad hard-boiled egg. In response to a letter in which Johnny had asked whether Ben had been for the Vikings or the Steelers in the most recent Super Bowl, Ben wrote in January 1975, "Of course I rooted for the Vikings, & I certainly hope they won. I assume from the name that the Steelers are from Pittsburgh, & I couldn't condone that. Where are the Vikings from? Oslo?"

In the fall of 1981, Johnny delivered one of a series of lectures entitled "Last Lectures" at Ouachita Baptist University. The idea was that one was to suppose that the talk represented the last opportunity to speak to a group, and, therefore, the topic would be one the speaker considered both important and representative of his or her thought. Johnny had urged that people should cultivate their curiosity, their desire to learn, and he illustrated his point early in his speech with a long list of items which might be interesting to know. The list included everything from Latin verb conjugations to plays run by the

Dallas Cowboys. He sent Ben a copy of the speech, and Ben declared it "A lovely talk—almost enough to induce me to be curious about the Dallas Cowboys." Later that fall, Ben had this to say: "To show you that I do have some curiosity, the Rams have just stunned the Cowboys."

His choice of the verb *stunned* is a giveaway that he had spotted a headline somewhere (he did not subscribe to or read any newspapers); he had a knack for remembering and echoing details not only of great literature but also of less exalted texts, such as advertisements, menus, and headlines. One Sunday morning when a number of us had gathered for the weekend in Little Rock, we met for breakfast; Jack had picked up a newspaper bearing the headline FANS DAZED AS HOGS FALL TO RICE. Later in the day, we were to meet some other people, one of whom Ben had never met. We were trying to prepare him for this encounter by telling him a little about the man, who was something of an eccentric, a vocal and rather volatile political liberal, and a rabid fan of the Arkansas Razorbacks. Duly warned, Ben said, "We won't have to worry about that; he'll be in a daze."

We all shared a distaste for: the practice, commonly observed in dressing rooms before a game, of praying to win. Having received from Johnny a report that two opposing teams had both been shown before the game praying for victory, and that, naturally, one of them had lost--a thumping defeat, in fact, Ben wrote, "I assume the Louisville Cardinals are now prepared to join me in asking the Almighty to stop intervening in things that don't concern him?"

On another occasion, Johnny had chided him for not having recognized the name of a well-known sportscaster. Ben responded, "I'll take your word for it that Harry Caray is famous, but he's obviously just one of those people who drink odd daiquiris. So much for him."

Toward the end of a considerably less than successful football season for the University of Arkansas team, the departure of the head coach appeared imminent, although, rather than being fired, this one was being tempted by a more lucrative position. As usual, Johnny was having fun discussing the subject with Ben in their correspondence. When the rumors of change first began circulating, Johnny forthwith informed Ben, as he normally did, by bringing it up casually in a tone that suggested that Ben would, of course, already know all about it, being vitally interested as he was in such matters. Ben always obliged Johnny by playing his games as he played all games--well and with interest and great gusto. Ben wrote, "I have twice this fall run from the house yelling, 'The season is ruined!' And now they say we may lose the son of a bitch who ruined it!" And in reference to the hefty increase in salary that was supposedly luring the coach away from Fayetteville, Ben defended him: "You & the *Gazette* have misunderstood him—he meant he couldn't live with himself on the salary he was making. Now he can afford to live with someone else—anyone he wants." When Johnny suggested that perhaps, then, the coach was considering the forty-percent increase only because he had been lonely, not having been able to afford to live with someone else on his salary, and that the situation might be remedied if someone would volunteer to be his companion. With the relative percentages of the two salaries in mind, Ben wrote, "I will try to find 3/5's of a suitable person for him to live with—I'm very much upset about his sad fate."

In his usual spirit of feigned innocence, Ben wrote the following letter in the summer of 1979 from New Haven, where he was working primarily on the Pound research:

> Dear Dr. Wink,
>
>   I hope that you can help me with a research problem in a field in which you have the reputation of being an expert. A book which I am teaching to freshmen next fall has an obscure reference to a game called "baseball" which, it appears, was played by Americans in the 1940s. One of the groups who played this game was called by the odd name of "Dodgers," and one of the "Dodgers" was a black man named "Jackie." A dim prompting in the back of my brain (which may be either divine inspiration or the promptings of the devil) suggests that his last name was Robertson, but I am by no means certain (the name Onassis also keeps suggesting it self) , & since there is a chance that one of my students might be an expert in this branch of learning (even on events so long ago) , I am afraid to risk it without confirmation. If you are unable to help me, perhaps you have a colleague familiar with the "Dodgers" to whom you could forward this letter.
>
> With sincere thanks for your trouble,
> Ben Kimpel

In addition to revealing one of the ways Ben played with the whole idea of sports, the foregoing letter illustrates other matters that bothered or puzzled him. He could never understand the popular interest in the private (or public, for that matter) life of Jacqueline Kennedy Onassis; notions of divine or satanic influence left him cold; and that an ever increasing number of his students knew nothing at all about even the relatively recent past disturbed him. The letter also shows his ability to play the scholar as well as be one. He did not reserve his satire for fields other than his own by any means; in fact, his attacks on his own profession were perhaps the sharpest of all.

He detested cant, and his discipline, like all others, had become full of it. He tended to blame both the advertising industry and some segments of academic community for what he perceived as the degeneration and devaluation of language. "He had a distaste," Lyell Behr has written of Ben, "for the social sciences which invent words for phenomena for which we already have good words and which change the meaning of good words we already have." The primary sin of advertisement, on the other hand, was a kind of word inflation, particularly of adjectives, in which "large" became "giant" or "colossal," and "good" was never good enough, but had to be "fantastic" or "miraculous" so that "large" and "good" had come to lose all their modifying force.

When it came to cant, Ben could be devastating, by either exposing it directly or exposing it indirectly through parody, as with "praying for the conversion of football," which mimics a kind of pious jargon which Ben detested, particularly because often it pretends to be charitable but is in fact vicious or, at best, condescending. His aversion to such hypocritical language was perhaps only slightly stronger than his aversion to pretentious language, which represents, after all, just another sort of deception. After Johnny had sent a copy of an essay by a prominent contemporary critic, Ben revealed his opinion of it in the following letter:

Dear Sir,

Thank you for the enlightening article. I have for many years been looking for a standard of literature & of contemporary morality the accepting or rejecting of which is no longer an option. I now discover that both consist in meditating, in the spirit but not the style of the Romantic lyric of crisis, on (at the same time) Poetry & Morality, & on how both depend on the mind which circles the subject (forever, without zeroing in) and remains "concerned with what our imagination makes of our ordinariness." What does your imagination make of your ordinariness?

Ben D. Kimpel
Ph.D. & Modernist

Ben often underlined his sardonic attacks on overblown rhetoric and ideas or theories that he considered dubious or nonsensical by signing his full name and adding his degree and some title or another, as with "Ph.D. & Modernist" above, but the real artistry of most of his satire resides in the body of the text itself. The letter quoted above demonstrates his ability to condense an idea—or what was posing as one--to a single, concise statement, using the language of the original, but using it in such a way as to reveal how absurd and how finally incoherent and imprecise he found it. And that concluding question is vintage Ben Kimpel.

Ben characterized his own approach to literature and literary criticism as "old-fashioned" and said with no small relief that he had finished his degrees just before "people started having theories." He read, understood, and occasionally referred to or explained the ideas of most of the schools of criticism which have sprung up in the twentieth century, but he relied on few if any of their methods in his own reading and teaching, or, at least, he did not consciously rely upon them. He also, in the appropriate courses, had his students read representative texts from some of the more influential schools of criticism. On the whole, however,

he rejected most of these critical notions because he simply did not find them very helpful, but, although many of the ideas of very recent criticism he found at best silly and at worst downright pernicious, he did grant them some validity, as the following excerpt concerning the teaching of composition courses from his Oxford Lecture shows:

> It seems to me that what composition courses ought to be doing is teaching people who have a thought—I don't know how to teach those people who don't—how to express that thought clearly and accurately, without using clichés, in such a way as to wake people up to what they're saying. I'm not saying this is what all composition courses do.
>
> In this way we're going against a very important trend in the modern world; among the suicidal tendencies in the English profession, I would say there is one very important one in critical theory now: that language never refers to anything outside itself. It's a self-contained system; there's no reference to any world outside of it.
>
> This is unfortunately true of a good many systems of language: political speeches, for instance, advertisements, the releases of public relations—they're not true, not false—they don't deal with anything. They're a certain series of words: "miraculous new wash powder." Obviously, that is not real. If that's the proper way to use language, then I'm not sure that we really want to teach freshman composition.

Ben placed a good deal of the blame for the proliferation of new and, to his thinking, by and large useless critical theories on an academic community which had come to insist upon publication from its members if they wished to advance in their profession and, more and more frequently, even if they wished to be employed. As far as Ben was concerned, publication should be one of the ways to teach, a way to disseminate what one has learned, but he felt that it was not necessarily something every teacher either can or should do. In his opinion, the pressure to publish placed on virtually everyone in the profession had the result, quite apart from the creation of a seemingly endless stream of very bad writing, of pushing scholarship too far toward specialization and the esoteric.

Before the all but universal demand for publication became established, his concerns for graduate students were different from what they were afterwards. According to Lyell Behr, Ben "deplored the situation of writers of Ph.D. dissertations in English who had to find some author who had been, and probably should be, forgotten, or else dig up minutiae of no consequence concerning those more famous." At that time he also allowed a great deal of flexibility in his courses insofar as the traditional term paper was concerned. He encouraged the unusual and the creative. In one course in which the students were required to write responses to the reading, Ben told the class that these papers could be ten pages or one line long. One of the students in that class has reported, "I decided to take him up on the challenge and write a one-sentence reaction paper on Camus' *The Stranger*. I worked days trying to come up with a brilliant sentence. I finally did something, turned it in with much trepidation, and Ben, of course, accepted it, realizing probably better than I the agony that had gone into putting it into one sentence." In a course in the literature of China and Japan, he accepted as term projects a Japanese tea ceremony and a series of illustrations of the novel *Monkey* and would have accepted the mustard seed that one student turned in except that, as Ben later told him, the student had been too apologetic, giving away that he did not believe in either the value of the symbol or the validity of his gesture.

The following anecdote provided by Russ Goodyear concerns a result of one instance of Ben's nontraditional approach:

> In the summer of 1970, I signed up for Medieval Germanic Literature with Kimpel. He wanted to be up-to-date, so he encouraged us to "projects" instead of the traditional paper. On the last day of the semester when the projects were due, one student had made mead. We all dutifully took a sip as the jug passed around the room and finally ended up on Dr. Kimpel's desk. As the class progressed, Ben took one sip after another. Soon a rosy glow spread across his cheeks and his lecture became more and more inspired. He was in fine form, and at the end of the class (and the mead!), in response to some worry wart who wanted to know what was going to be on the final exam, Ben leapt to his feet and shouted, "We ought to fight it out with swords for a grade, just the way the Vikings did it!"

All in all, it was one of the best Kimpel classes in my experience.

He would accept conventional papers, of course, and occasionally would require them, but in many of his courses he had a more or less open policy which he hoped would encourage creative, original thought. That changed as the situation surrounding the profession changed. Even though he had himself a relatively impressive body of published scholarship, he had opposed, without success, the adoption of publication as one of the primary criteria for promotion of the English faculty at Fayetteville, but he saw that for his graduates it was quickly becoming a necessity. As soon as he realized that to publish while still in graduate school was in the students' best interest, he began to require more formal research papers in his courses.

He did not, however, like the emphasis on publication or much of what it produced. Of one particular group of modern critics he said disdainfully, "They like to make up terms and then argue about what they mean." In our correspondence, he made a number of comments about one such term:

> I have now seen the word "intertextuality" in type, if not in print, and I do not feel that my life is the richer. . . . I will soon have tidings of great joy (I hope) regarding intertextuality—I am beginning Derrida's On *Grammatology*, which must mention it. I feel sure that (with some caution) it can be practiced openly even in a Baptist U. Our highly respected new critical theorist is reported to do it. I want you to appreciate the fact that an age even more crabbed than yours is trying to learn something new. I also just read a book on Ezra Pound by a disciple of Jacques Lacan & now call all phrases signifiers. . . . Derrida had nothing on intertextuality (-ism?). I now hear that I should have tried someone named Raffatiere [sic]. If he's like Derrida, I won't. But he can't be—Derrida is unique (I trust).
>
> . . . To show you that mentees, if good or only mildly rebellious, get rewarded by getting answers to their questions: Intertexuality is a method of assuring that every poem which fits the true definition of the genre "poetry" can get a double (& conflicting) reading, a heuristic reading which discovers the "meaning" on the level of mimesis & a hermeneutic reading which discovers the "significance" on the (deeper) level of semiosis. Intertexts may be quotations from or allusions to other literary works, but they may also be proverbs or cliches. They function as puns function, to create a catachresis or ungrammaticality which alerts the reader worth his salt that he is getting to

the crux of the matter. Intertextual reading answers the main purpose of reading poetry by assuring us that what we think is the "meaning" is important (except as contrast) only to the nonelite. The "significance" is always the same: poetry refers only to itself & is a game with words, a game of infinite interest. I trust that clears things up?

Ben, of course, cheerfully threw in his lot with the "nonelite." His lack of sympathy with many modern theorists had at least as much to do with how they used language as with what they said about language. Conversely, his respect for earlier critics, such as Empson or Brooks, depended largely on their having been good prose stylists in their own right. He may not have agreed with their premises, but he admired the clarity with which they were expressed. Some have perceived Ben's attitudes toward some contemporary trends in criticism as having been much too conservative, even backward-looking. However just that evaluation may be, one can be relatively sure that Ben approached these writers and their ideas with as little prejudice and as open a mind as one is likely to encounter in any reader.

Among the results, or perhaps the bases, of Ben's conservatism—which extended far beyond his attitudes toward modern critical theory and is explored elsewhere in this book—was that he was very suspicious of the idea of progress, especially in the forms it has tended to take in our century—such forms as, for example, canned biscuits and frozen pie crusts. And gadgetry, technological and otherwise, irked him. He detested hot-air hand dryers, clever salt and pepper shakers, lavatory fixtures featuring a single knob, and a host of other "innovations." Many a time he would return to a restaurant table and launch into a scathing satire of 20th-century gadgetry, triggered by his having been forced to use one of those loathsome hot-air blowers. "I know, why don't we invent a bar that a cloth towel can be hung over, or, if not that, a metal holder with paper towels in it?" A rather baroque salt-and-pepper dispenser once led him to suggest the invention of "two small glass bottles, one for salt and one for pepper, with metal caps with holes in them, and if you want salt, you just turn it over and shake out what you want." He had a plan to make millions with plumbing fixtures: two separate spouts, one for hot water and one for cold, "with handles that you twist to turn them on and off, and if you want to mix them together, you could do that with, oh, say a little rubber stopper."

One of the first comments on the idea of progress I heard him make concerned the idea that our century represents an improvement over the Middle Ages. Ben was quick to question that as an unqualified assumption by asking the class how many could identify more than three constellations. Very few could. His point was that, in the Middle Ages, anyone who was educated could have identified them all. "So, in what sense have we progressed?"

His impatience with gadgets extended to many things that most people consider necessities, such as telephones and televisions. I think in both of those cases, however, Ben's hatred stemmed more from their abuse than from their existence. For years and years, Ben refused to have a television in his home, but finally began thinking of buying one, saying, "I've come down from never to 1980." It was some programming on the public or educational channel that tipped the scales: a promising dramatization of a novel, productions of Shakespeare, or a series on art. In any case, he finally bought a television, a rather large one, in fact, which was placed in the front spare bedroom of his home. Although he eventually subscribed to two of the so-called movie channels, he continued to watch television very sparingly, even putting the names of shows he wanted to see in his appointment book, and when he was watching he would do nothing else and brooked no interruptions. If the phone rang, he would let it ring; someone who was watching a program with him once when the phone rang asked if Ben would like for him to answer it. "No," Ben said flatly, "if it's important, they'll call back."

He was consciously indebted to a good deal of 20th-century technology, however. Obviously, he owed much of the richness and pleasure of his life to jet propulsion. His favorite appliance, according to his sister, Betty Warner, was the garbage disposal, a fact which surprised me until, upon reflection, I realized that someone who is not concerned with feeding a compost pile could find a disposal unit something other than a noisy nuisance. He also considered the vacuum cleaner something of an improvement over the broom and dustpan. As I have already mentioned, Ben used his vacuum cleaner about once a week, generally on Saturday morning. Johnny witnessed this ritual one week-end when he was staying with Ben, and, because Johnny was there and was trailing around after him talking, Ben did not put his opera on that morning. Johnny has described him, still in his pajamas, moving very briskly around the rooms, quickly covering every floor in his house, and responding to Johnny's chatter. The evening before, Duncan had been talking about eighteenth-century periodicals and the questions that were sent in as letters to the editor. One question that amused Duncan was, "Will Negroes rise on Judgment Day?" Johnny repeated the question to Ben that morning as Ben doggedly pushed the vacuum cleaner about his house. "Why should they? Why should they want to?" Ben responded; "I don't want to rise on Judgment Day;" and after a pause, "Come to think of it, I didn't particularly want to rise this morning!"

Ben's vacuum cleaner was an older model which his sister had given him. Once on a visit to her brother in Fayetteville, she discovered that the hose had an enormous hole in it, which, because of its size, she judged had been there for quite some time. There's no telling for how long Ben had been rising reluctantly on Saturday mornings and dutifully rearranging the dust in his house.

Aside from airplanes, vacuum cleaners, garbage disposal units, and, of course, the automobile, he considered the worth of much modern technology dubious, at best. As it applied to his own field, the computer seemed to him a mere gewgaw, and he staunchly refused to learn to use one. He could not see that computers offered to the writer or researcher any advantage over a typewriter or the card catalogue. This resistance to the use of electronic devices extended even to calculators, as the following story told by one of his colleagues demonstrates:

> Just at the time when he became departmental chairman the floodgates of bureaucratic paperwork in the university really opened--up until then, the university had not got modern, that is to say it was not mired calf-deep in paper of its own making and spoil age, but it happened just about then. There was an incredible amount of periodic reporting that had to be done by every budget officer, and that includes the chairman.

> A lot of the stuff had to be done every month, four or five different sorts of annual reports had to be done, and at the end of each semester and each summer term were all sorts of housekeeping details, and much of this included in large amount canonical numbers of various sorts. Well, I discovered to my horror one day that Ben was doing most of that himself, doing all the computations by hand. He was making tallies with, you know, four vertical strokes and one angular stroke, but then they had to be added together in various ingenious ways and divided by other numbers and things like that--and he was doing all of that by hand. I was appalled.

> I suggested that a calculator would surely be faster. Well, he didn't much like the idea; he didn't trust them very much, he said, and, anyway, he didn't know how to use one.

> So I bought him one, a printing calculator, and brought it in, showed him how to use it, and refused to leave his office until he had done a couple of simple sums to prove that he could indeed do it. And I said, "Now you can do on this all those calculations that you've been doing on scratch paper by hand." "Yes, yes, mm-hmm, I can do that," he said.

> Well, that was the last I saw of the calculator for a while, and then later on I saw him doing some more adding and subtracting on scraps of paper with stubby pencils, so I asked him about it, and he said that somebody

had stolen it out of his desk drawer. Now, I didn't care one way or another, but I told him I thought he had probably thrown it away in exasperation, and he said no he hadn't, and I said well, it's gone anyway, and he said yes, it's too bad, it's certainly gone. So I got him another one.

I saw him use that one a few times afterwards, but I'd be willing to bet that he waited until he knew I was in the hall close to his office, and then he'd dig the thing out and make a show of punching numbers into it so that I would see him using it.

Had he been born even perhaps as few as ten years later than he was, doubtless he would have accepted computers and calculators and used them, as he did the airplane, for example, to their full advantage. Yet it seems somehow redundant to lament the fact that a man who used his time so efficiently that he read more, traveled more, and, in general, accomplished more than most could in several lifetimes did not take advantage of a few time-saving devices. "Just think what he could have done" sounds rather silly when realizing all that he actually did is difficult enough.

Claude Gibson has echoed the sentiments of many in writing that Ben's "vivacity gave him an aura of invincibility which made the news of his death extremely shocking; until that it was difficult to accept Ben Kimpel as a mere mortal." And even for those who accepted him as mortal, there was something: as Richard Marius has written, "We all knew he would kill himself with his drinking and smoking and eating, but we all supposed that it would be after we had all passed to dust." Not only Ben's physical stamina and splendid energies but also his kindness, generosity, good nature, intelligence, wit, and all the other good qualities contributed to feelings that he was in some sense superhuman. In all the interviews and correspondence connected with this biography, nothing has shown more clearly how pervasive these feelings were among his friends and acquaintances than the frequency of such phrases as "it's important to remember that he was not perfect" and "he was, after all, human" or "he was not without his faults." It is interesting that those of us who knew him must keep reminding ourselves and each other of so obvious a fact. One of the questions I routinely asked at interviews concerned what people saw as his flaws or his failings. Not one person was able to answer the question without a great deal of reflection, and many simply could not think of anything at all. The way Professor Marius has phrased it is telling: "Ben had his flaws. One has to say that, though when I do, I feel almost disloyal." As Ben's biographer, I have struggled with that feeling of disloyalty; whenever I sense that some revelation may leave a negative impression, something in me wants to rush forth and qualify it, justify it, rectify it—not because he was perfect—he was not—but because, first, for all who knew him, the good about him so far outweighed the bad, and, second—and, I think, even more compelling—he was himself so rarely judgmental, "so generous in his estimation of others," as Lyna Lee Montgomery has said.

However, it really is important to remember that he was not perfect, that he was human, and that he was not without his faults. Again I turn to Richard Marius, who has expressed so well and so provocatively what he perceived as Ben's flaws:

> . . . One was basic; the others were much less important. The basic flaw was that he tried to know too much. I never found him interested in interpreting a literary work. Now and then I would ask him a question that involved interpretation, and I always felt that seemed uncomfortable with any sort of speculation or inference. He was much more at ease discussing the facts, what was in the text. In all the years I knew him, he never said anything about a text that made me see it in a different way, made me suddenly perceive a meaning in it that I had not thought before. Great critics like Cleanth Brooks or Bill Wimsatt or Helen Vendler have the power to tell us something about a text that we can never forget once we have read their interpretation of it. Ben did not have that power, probably because he did not have any interest in such matters. When I consider his intelligence, his amazing breadth of knowledge, I find it sad that he left so little writing. His biography of Richardson is a contribution of merit, but I was never interested enough in it to read it through. I wish he had read less and thought more about what he did read and that he had written about texts in the way he never did.

> He commanded so much information that he could seem overpowering, and at times he liked to overpower people. Sometimes he was wrong. Lanier [Marius's wife] was a student in art history at Mississippi State College for Women before I met her and before I was on the committee. She came up to be interviewed in Memphis. Ben took the lead in questioning her, and because she had traveled in Italy, he asked her about various art works of the Italian renaissance. He asked her about a crucifixion by Masaccio in Florence. She said that it was not a crucifixion but that it was a painting of the Trinity. Ben insisted that it was a crucifixion. It did show Christ on the cross, but the painting was of the Trinity. Last Monday night we were watching the art history series on Channel Two, and the painting came up. "That's the painting Ben flunked me on for a Woodrow Wilson." The commentator described it as a Trinity.

She came to like Ben enormously, but she still recalls how unwilling he was to consider that he might have made an error. I found him very much like that in all his judgments. He could never imagine that the United States was committing horrors in Vietnam. We had some fierce arguments about the validity of our war there. Ben said that war was war, that it was cruel, and that it was foolish to imagine that it could be any other way. If we were going to fight a war, we had to be willing to be cruel. I led the anti-war movement in East Tennessee and probably, if the truth be known, in just about the whole state. Ben never opposed the war, though he did support the right of others to oppose it. There was no give in him, no willingness to reconsider an opinion, and those of us who talk with some give and take about issues were always at a disadvantage when we argued with him. We might reconsider our opinions, but Ben never reconsidered his. He liked other people, but I could never see that he had compassion or even sympathy for other human beings. It was perhaps something he had walled away inside that could not get out.

Sometimes that got in the way of interviewing [for the Woodrow Wilson Fellowships]. One time we were talking to a country boy from the mountainous region of middle Tennessee. He had been to Tennessee Tech, studying history. I took the lead in questioning him. I asked him a question about Reconstruction. He leaned forward and said, "Now, you take the nigger." Ralph [Norman] and I were the liberal members of the committee. Ben and Lyell [Behr] were the conservatives. Ralph and I saw that we had a very bright boy who had not been educated. Ben and Lyell heard the word "nigger" and resolved to throw him down to hell. We debated fiercely, and I finally used my prerogative as chairman to give him the fellowship. He went to Princeton to graduate school, did outstanding work, returned to Tennessee Tech, has become one of the luminaries there, and thanks me every time I see him for giving him a chance.

As I have indicated, Ben liked people, but he was extraordinarily self-sufficient. I suppose that he lived for his books, his learning. I saw him for the last time when he came to Harvard to do some work on Pound. One afternoon I walked through the big reading room in Widener and looked down the ranks of tables and saw the back of a familiar white-haired man. I walked over with incredulous caution and said, "Ben?" He looked up. I greeted him with great warmth, and discovered that he had been there for a week. Lanier and I had him to dinner and with several others at the table had a witty, delightful evening. Later I took him to lunch with a couple of younger men interested in Pound and reverent at Ben's command of the information. He was resolved, he said, to learn every allusion in the *Cantos*. I said afterwards to Lanier that I wondered if Ben would have made any effort to reach me had I not stumbled on him by accident in the Widener. I could not tell whether he wanted to be with people or whether he merely tolerated us. I often wondered if he feared to impose himself, perhaps thinking that he might offend if he presumed that others wanted him around. He almost never wrote letters, though now and again he would send a card or a note. He was not a man to sit down and pour himself out on paper. I think he had a great capacity for affection, but I suppose that he always felt a little uneasy in expressing it. I never saw it.

From time to time before Ben became chairman of the English department at the University and much more frequently during his tenure as chairman, he was involved in sometimes bitter conflicts, either within the department or between the department and the administration. He did not like confrontation and had usually managed to avoid it until he was made chairman, at which time confrontation often became unavoidable. Jessie O'Kelly has said that "the conflicts in the English department bothered him no end, but that didn't indicate anything wrong with Ben; it was just the kind of thing he couldn't stand to cope with." But cope he did for seven years as chairman, bringing to the job, according to a friend and colleague, "an acute ability to identify when one really needed to take a stand. And as chairman, he had to take many stands, but he always gave alternatives. I can't think of a situation when he said if we don't get this, it's the end of this."

Because final decisions were often his responsibility as chairman, however, and almost no final decision is likely to satisfy everyone, Ben frequently found himself in conflict with one or more members of his department or, as the official spokesman of his department, with the administration.

Bringing the force of his intelligence and wit to bear in an argument, Ben could be a formidable opponent, and he could be ruthless. He rarely lost his temper, but when he did, he was not above yelling at people or resorting to what one observer has called "schoolyard tactics" ("probably a reflection," it was added, "of the last time in his life that he had had to use them").

During the time he was chairman, Ben found one particular administrator especially troublesome in that he frustrated Ben's wishes and those of the department time after time. Ben used to return from interviews with him red-faced and irritable, and once he exclaimed, "I think I like that man as little as any man I've ever known!" I heard this story from several people, every one of whom commented on the way Ben had phrased the statement—not "I dislike that man" but "I like him as little"—as an indication of Ben's unconscious habit of perceiving even the most unpleasant things in the most positive light possible.

In his Oxford Lecture, discussing the three areas in which professors are measured, Ben had this to say about one of them:

> The second field, service, is not really much help if you want to become a college teacher or a researcher, though it's probably the best way on earth to get to the top financially. What it does, of course, eventually, for people who put tremendous stress on service, is to take them out of teaching altogether and into administration, which I would say—I'm paying a compliment to some of the administrators I've known—seems to me somewhat of a shame. I think they were too good to be administrators and would have done perfectly well to have gone on as teachers--but they've got more money out of it.

Given this attitude, it is not difficult to understand that he did not enjoy being an administrator himself. Opinions vary concerning Ben's feelings about being chairman; some think that, although he did not hunger to be chairman, he was happy enough to accept the post; others believe he took the job rather reluctantly, out of a sense of duty; but the opinions of those closest to him are best expressed by Jessie O'Kelly: "He didn't want to be chairman at all." According to what he told us at the time that Claude Faulkner stepped down as chairman in 1974, Ben took the job only because he was the only choice that various factions within the department could agree upon. And he continued to serve as long as he did for the same reason.

The following comments from one of his colleagues may suggest several reasons why he was the most widely accepted candidate for the job among the members of the faculty:

> He was one who did his best to release the constructive energies of those with whom he was associated. That best characterizes his service as chairman and as a member of this department. He certainly was not naïve about the weaknesses of other people, but he worked to their strengths as much as possible, and that's the best characteristic of a leader.

And he did it quietly, too. And he did it informally; there aren't many formal memoranda from Ben Kimpel, and that, I think, shows a respect for people. I had scores of notes from him, sometimes on the back of an envelope: "What do you think about this?" "Spring schedules due in two weeks—at least we have two weeks this time!"—things like that—just scratch paper. He never made a big project out of something that didn't need to be a big project.

Ben was generally able to leave any unpleasantness associated with his job behind him when he was away from it, but during his tenure as chairman he seemed troubled by or preoccupied with some problem confronting him in connection with his work more often than before. His reactions to these problems varied: he brooded about some, others triggered a kind of low-key anger, to some he reacted as he would have to a bad meal, but most of them simply either annoyed or exasperated him. He was clearly not enamoured of the job. He wanted to resign a number of times before he finally did; but, according to one member of the department, "he stayed on out of that strength of his, loyalty—feeling loyalty to the people in the department--and feeling that he could still accomplish something."

The chairmanship put a strain on Ben as it would on anyone who took its responsibilities seriously, but many of his friends felt that the reasons it affected Ben as it did were different from what they might be for most other people. The following evaluation of Ben's problems with being chairman reflects an attitude widely held among his friends and colleagues:

> Ben was in some ways a kind of innocent; he always wanted to see the best in everybody. Before he was chairman, he had been a compromiser in the department; if there were two views of things, very frequently he would be the one who would propose a solution that would be at least satisfactory for each side, with each having to yield some. But as chairman, you've got to act; you've got to make a decision, and whichever way you go is going to make one person or one group of people unhappy.
>
> I think Ben really had the view that if you want to help people, if your intentions are good and you want to do the best you can for them, that people will be pleased. And after he became chairman he found that isn't true. He found that you can't please people, and I think this really did distress him a lot. He wanted to be fair, to do the best he could, and give every opportunity, and treat everybody right, and he felt that if you did that, then

everyone would be happy, and then he found, sort of like Rasselas and what Rasselas finds out, that even the most benevolent ruler can't make people happy. With Ben, I think there was a disillusionment with that.

Ben believed that if people knew that your heart was good and that you meant to be fair and just and as benevolent as you knew how to be, then people would accept that and be appreciative. That was part of his charm; because he was appreciative and tried to see the best in everyone, that's the way he perceived everyone else, too. And it distressed him so much when people were unhappy and there wasn't any way he could go to prevent it. I think that was a problem with his chairmanship; it troubled him. Nobody had ever been mad at him before, and I expect that people came and complained and were angry about decisions that he had made that he had to make. It's strange to get to be sixty years old before you realize that you can't make everybody happy, and I think Ben really thought he could.

His resignation became effective in July 1981. Because of Ben's gift for being able to be engaged in and enjoy whatever he happened to be doing, he had not exactly hated his post as chairman, but it is likely that, during many periods in the seven years he served, he had prayed daily for its conversion.

CHAPTER EIGHT

"I understand it in principle. You come back as a hedgehog." He sucked on his cigarette and quickly exhaled. "But what comes back as a hedgehog?"

We were seated in the dimly-lit bar of the Florida restaurant in Juarez, waiting for our table: Jack Butler, Johnny Wink, Susan Wink, and Ben Kimpel. It's one of the clearest of perhaps a hundred clear images of Ben that bump around in my head all the time, some one or another flasping unexpectedly on my mind's eye almost every day and triggering a rapid succession of memories-like a slideshow.

We were talking, obviously, about reincarnation; Ben's question, as Ben's questions often were, was really a statement: any aspect of his being in the continuation of which beyond death he had any interest at all could not possibly exist in a hedgehog. Looking at him that night, I couldn't help imagining him a huge, cigarette-smoking, bespectacled hedgehog. My fancies aside, I thought, "No--it's this or nothing. He can't come back as a hedgehog. It wouldn't be Ben."

He said that if there were such a thing as reincarnation, he'd like to come back as a tulip. And he has, he does—at least insofar as none of us to whom he said that can see a tulip without thinking of him. In that sense, he comes back as a thousand things: any work of Joyce, Milton, Pound, Proust, Yeats or a hundred other writers; Botticelli, the Black Hills, and biscuits; cactus flowers, Camel cigarettes, cardinal flowers, cheeseburgers, columbines, Confucius, and cornstarch; Dewar's Scotch, the Everglades, France, foot bridges, fresh trout, fried chicken, and frozen peach daiquiris; Gilbert and Sullivan, Glacier National Park, goldfish, and the Grand Tetons; Isle Royal, hedgehogs, lamb, limericks, and New Hampshire license plates; maidenhair fern, margaritas, Michelangelo, Monument Valley, and Mozart; opera, panther suits, and pastel colors; redbud trees, the Rockies, and Russian vodka; Santa Fe, Smokey the Bear, and strong coffee; the Viennese waltz and Zion. And that's only a tiny portion of the list.

While I was in school, my relationship to Ben was very like that of other graduate students who admired him. I took him for every course that I could; hardly a semester passed that I did not take at least one course from him. I stood in awe of him, I was tongue-tied around him, and I was terrified of disappointing him--something that, in my egoism, I failed to recognize would have been very difficult to do. The seminar in Yeats that I had from him met once a week at night in a classroom in one wing of Old Main; one evening another member of the English faculty had come up to his office for something, and, as he passed the open door of our classroom, he heard Ben's voice booming out. "Ego dominus tuus," Ben was saying. And, indeed, many of us thought he was.

When Johnny and I married in the spring of 1969, we invited very few people to our wedding. We wanted very much for Ben to be there, but it was during the spring break, and Ben, as was his wont, had made plans months in advance. He was in Nicaragua on the day of the wedding, and his reservations had probably been made before Johnny and I had gone out on our first date.

During the 1969-70 school year, Ben was at Harvard studying, primarily, Chinese. He came to Fayetteville for a visit some time that year—around Christmas as I recall. He had someone living in his house, and so he stayed the two or three days that he was in town at the Holiday Inn. Four or five of us--Johnny and I, John Calhoun, Rex Stamper, I think, and perhaps one or two others-went out to visit him. He was a little depressed that day. I don't remember exactly what he said, but I know that he was finding Chinese devilishly hard and he seemed to me to be a little frightened. He made some allusion to his age (he was only fifty-four) and the possibility that he was losing some of his ability to learn. Ben was one of the bravest men I've ever known--as Richard Marius said of him, "Ben had a sense of resignation in life; what was to be would be. He never flinched before danger"—but, before the danger of losing his mental and intellectual powers, I saw him flinch—once—briefly.

When our son, Gene, was born in January 1970, Ben was back in Cambridge. Johnny wrote him with the news of Gene's birth, ending his letter with Ivan Ilych's exclamation, "What joy!" We received in return our first letter--well, hardly a letter really—from Ben:

> Dear John & Susan—
> I suppose in spite of the population explosion I can still say "congratulations"—one is safely within ZPG.
> "What Joy!" I hope for Gene—
> Ben K.
> See you next month.

Johnny and I left Fayetteville in August 1973 and moved some two hundred miles south to Arkadelphia, where Johnny had accepted a position in the English department at Ouachita Baptist University. We were happy that one of us had found a job—that was about the time that the Great Iron Doors of employment were closing rapidly for college teachers; many of us squeezed through at the last minute, horribly maimed, but alive—but leaving Fayetteville was difficult, one of the main reasons being that, finally, after years of wishing it to be so, we were beginning to feel like real friends of Ben Kimpel's. We hated to leave him. We never dreamed of what was to come in our relationship with him.

I owe the great pleasure of my friendship with Ben from 1974 until his death to Johnny Wink—engaging, open, unselfconscious, and unpretentious Johnny Wink—and to his great love for Ben. He was not going to let Ben go out of our lives without finding out first whether or not it had to be that way. Ben was the director of Johnny's dissertation on John Cheever, and, since the final draft of the dissertation was not finished when we left Fayetteville, the two continued to correspond with each other on a quasi-official basis until Johnny received his Ph.D. in January 1974. I say "quasi-official" because both Johnny and Ben began almost immediately to mix a little nonsense with their business, as the following letter dated October 1973 shows:

> Dear Johnny,
>
> I don't find Gilbert on the list of suggested papers (Cranes Crest Bond, Lancaster Bond, Old Hampshire Bond, Oriole Linen Bond, and Permanized Parchment Bond) nor can I read the words 11 100% Cotton" (or "rag") by holding it up to the light. This is of major moment, the only thing that is. If your paper is identified as 100% cotton bond, it's OK; but be sure it is. The type looks fine, and the erasure of "stories" will, I think, get past--and even the centipede.
>
> Cordially,
>
> BK

Although in many of our letters from Ben I have no idea to what whimsy of Johnny's he is (whimsically) responding, I do know about the centipede. Johnny and I had recently read Alain Robbe-Grillet's Jalousie in which an image of the stain of a squashed centipede on a wall recurs; Johnny had undoubtedly suggested that such a stain appeared on one of the pages of his freshly typed thesis.

By January 1975, this sort of thing had gone on long enough for Johnny to do something that, a year earlier, he would never have thought he could do: he asked Ben for a loan. When we first came to Arkadelphia, we lived in an apartment. We had lived in a small but comfortable house in Fayetteville for several years and were frankly spoiled: in that apartment in Arkadelphia we felt as if we were living in a motel room and hardly unpacked for five months. As soon as we could, we bought a house. Johnny was actually making less at Ouachita than he had made as a graduate assistant, and I was bringing in no income at all, so the down payment and closing costs were something of a problem. But we needed only $1000 above what we were able to handle ourselves. We borrowed $500 from Johnny's father. Johnny wrote Ben for the other $500. We knew that he had lent and given a great deal of money to students and ex-students over the years. We didn't know it from him, however; he very often gave money anonymously, but even when his gifts were not anonymous, he never said a word about any of them. After Ben's death, Duncan Eaves told me that over a period of time Ben had periodically given him checks to cash and asked him to make up some story about where the money was coming from and pass the money on to a former student who had fallen on hard times. For whatever reason, Ben did not want the student to know that the money was from him. As far as I know, that person never knew the money was from Ben—Duncan successfully concocted a plausible story to account for it. It also occurs to me that any number of people who are reading this may think they were the student in question. such was Ben's generosity.

To Johnny's request, Ben replied simply, "No sweat--I just had a pleasant surprise on 1973 income tax" and sent us a $500 check. We repaid him very quickly. The correspondence continued. He almost always addressed his letters to both of us and opened them "Dear J & S." But the actual contents of the letters are directed to Johnny because it was Johnny who wrote to him--I think I wrote to Ben only once, the night before I taught my first class at Ouachita in the fall of 1974. It was in December of that fall that Ben first visited us in Arkadelphia. During those years, the OBU drama department was flourishing under the leadership of the very talented director and playwright Dennis Holt, whose reputation had attracted to Ouachita some of the best young actors in the state. In the fall of 1974, Dennis produced one of his own plays, *The Last Bouquet*, and it went on to all but sweep the awards in state and regional competitions. We asked Ben to come down for one of the performances. When he wrote Ben to invite him down, Johnny sent him one of his poems that involved a fanciful image based on Ben's having visited Ulan Bator, and, in his response to the first letter below, he forwarded a copy of a publication called *The Stone Drum*, in which the first of Johnny's published poems appeared.

Dear John and Susan,

Yes, I will try to get down for the play; assuming it's on a week-end, I don't see why I can't. I'd like to see all of you.

The Ulan Bator poem is worth at least $300—posterity may consider this estimate ludicrously inadequate. I only feel a little cheated that when my plane landed there, no one was there in a trenchcoat taking many pictures. But perhaps He has my photo.

If you hadn't avoided my courses so [Johnny took no fewer than seven courses from Ben], you'd have had a chance to hear me talk about *Cousine Bette, The Black Sheep,* & *Splendeurs & Miseries of Courtesans.* I read the whole *Human Comedy* 10-15 years ago in a (comparative for such a big work) rush, with almost constant enthusiasm. Insofar as the novel is about people doing interesting things, I don't think he's been beat. Try *Lost Illusions* next.

Tell Jack I've been enjoying the poems. I'm sorry his publication luck (after the repeated glory of *The New Yorker*) has temporarily declined. But I'm glad he's discovered Faulkner as you've discovered Balzac. He's picked two of the best of the stories.

Hope you all get up Thanksgiving & that I see you.

BK

Dear Johnny--

Hasty answer, to say I've gotten an announcement that your play is the week ending Sat., Dec. 7. I have an oral Sat. A.M., but if it's OK with you I'll drive down that afternoon.

I will be around F'v Thanksgiving (maybe not Thursday, but Friday). We can discuss mythology.

Thanks for *Stone Drum.* Is this your first printed work? A valuable bibliographical item--not to mention a good poem.

Best to Jack & Susan; hope to see you all T'giving.

BK

We did not make it to Fayetteville over the Thanksgiving holiday, but Ben did come down for the play, after which we sat at the kitchen table talking for hours. We gave him the only decent bed in the house. He went back to Fayetteville the following afternoon, taking with him the manuscript of what would eventually be Johnny's first published volume of poems. We received his Christmas card a few days later:

Thanks again for the good week-end--especially the talk. I've been through the poems twice with pleasure & will go through them again. Maybe "Stink-Fed Clams" is the high point, but I like all the Wayne poems about as much, & "Small Kafkaesque" & "The Attack of the P.E. coaches." "Lady Beatrice" is a joy. As a matter of fact, there are a good many joys, & a nice personal voice.

Ben's students, ex-students, friends, and colleagues so valued his opinion and advice that a not insignificant portion of his reading time was spent on various manuscripts that people had given him. With very few exceptions, he accepted these manuscripts willingly--even cheerfully, and he read them with care and attention. His comments, as they were on term papers and thesis chapters, were usually very brief--Doug Howard has said that, like so many others whose dissertations Ben directed (forty-eight in all; he was second or third reader on at least as many more), he could be fueled for weeks by a simple "Good—just go on like this" scrawled in Ben's hand across the first page of a chapter. In addition to the work of Jack Butler and Johnny, Ben read and helped Phil McMath with the final revisions of his novel, *Native Ground*; he read hundreds, perhaps thousands, of pages of Bill Meyer's poetry, and God only knows how much more.

Shortly after the first of the year in 1975, Johnny wrote Ben inviting him down for another play. He also sent him another "Ben" poem, asked him, with his usual talent for mixing up the world, what team he rooted for in the Super Bowl (Ben's response to this is quoted in Chapter 7 above) and what he thought about the Resurrection, and, screwing his courage to the sticking point, ventured to ask Ben if he would consider going on a trip with him and Jack Butler, who, in the fall of 1974, had moved to Arkadelphia from Jasper, Texas. Ben responded promptly:

> In spite of the flattering poem, I can only regard it as a disaster that anyone's handwriting should resemble mine.
>
> Don't know why I couldn't get to Arkadelphia for *The Tempest*--now that I know how to get from 14th St. to 14th St, it's an easy trip. Nor do I see why a trip to Yuma or the Chesapeake is out of the question. There are lots of places I want to see--Appalachia, Santa Fe & vicinity again after many years, southern Utah, northern Michigan (I was in camp there in 1926!! & haven't been back).
>
> I really don't think my opinion about the resurrection is worth anything. Everything you say I have knocked around, and I wish I knew. Unfortunately, there are too many miracles vouched for in various religions by presumably honest people. I *can't* really say I'm sure on someone else's hearsay. I could say it's *symbolically* true, & at one time I thought that a meaningful answer, but I'm not very happy with it now. The only thing I

know we can test is words we can try to apply--we can test those by the effect when we half-way succeed in applying them. It certainly is relevant whether there was really a resurrection, but whether or not, the Sermon on the Mount is there, in spite of the re-directed energy, which led to its being ignored pretty quickly. It was committed to time & is still safely there--just as Shakespeare is there in spite of schoolteachers & theatre audiences. Nietzsche was admired by the Nazis, but he can still be read. Time seems a moderately safe guardian, though ideas (& art) are probably always distorted when done in a comic-book version for· people not really interested but wanting a few shreds of culture or religion.

I gained disgracefully over Christmas but have lost it all back & am going on. If I appear in Arkadelphia around May 1, I'll weigh under 200--D.V. Look back on the week-end in Arkadelphia with great pleasure.

BK

And so it began. By April Ben was in high gear, engaged as he was in one of his very favorite things: the anticipation of a trip. He was like a child waiting for Christmas. They decided on Santa Fe; Ben immediately got to work on an itinerary. Early in April, the following notes arrived in rapid succession [This was on yellow notebook paper]:

1. For approval, disapproval, or alteration:

Sat. May 17		about Amarillo (from Ft. S., 453 m.)
Sun.	18	Santa Fe 289 m.
Mon	19	” ” Acoma (125 m.) & back
Tues	20	” ” Bandelier
Wed	21	” ”
Thurs	22	Taos 70 m.
Fri	23	” our pilgrimage to the great man's [D. H. Lawrence's] grave
Sat	24	Carlsbad 157 m. cavern in the P.M.
Sun	25	” Guadalupe Mts. (69 m.) & back
Mon	26	Alamogordo [sic] _(White Sands) 285 m.
Tues	27	about Abilene 399 m.
Wed	28	Ft. s. via Dallas 464 m.

2. I am prepared to write for any reservations desired.
3. When is *The Tempest*?
4. I continue to like the poems.

ITER - road
genitive ITINERIS,
whence itinerary
    BK

First (reverse play) the bad news—during the period in which I'd forgotten the date of *The Tempest*, I made arrangements to go to Kansas city May 3 for the Chinese exhibit. Tried to change, but Duncan has an exam the only other possible date, May 10.

The good news—I've written the two La Fondas, Santa Fe & Taos, and since the other towns seemed to offer no hotels of distinction I called the Holiday Inn for (& got) reservation at Amarillo May 17, Alamogordo [sic] May 24, Carlsbad May 25, San Angelo May 26--note change in itinerary, which now reads Mon., May 26, Carlsbad to San Angelo via Guadalupe Mts. 407 m., Tues., May 27, San Angelo--Jasper 433 m. Right?

Dear Johnny--
I got you and Jack a double room. OK?

I checked on *iter* in my Latin diet. to be sure. Of course I remembered the exact distance from San Angelo to Jasper, but I checked on that too, like the careful scholar I am, with Rand McNally.

    BK

The trip was a great success, a couple of very bad meals and a twice-broken-down Buick in Fort Stockton, Texas, notwith-standing. In New Mexico, in addition to walking in the snow to D.H. Lawrence's shrine, Ben seemed intent upon visiting every pueblo within driving distance of their route. At the age of fifty-nine, he was climbing high, steep trails and very precarious ladders up to and into kivas. Jack and Johnny were sometimes terrified for their lives; Ben never. He hadn't the least fear of heights, although on one especially treacherous descent from a kiva, he said, "I hope Johnny falls so a rescue unit will come." And about a small group of tourists gathered below one of the long ladders at Bandelier, he said, "They're down there just waiting for one of us to fall, goddam 'em. Look at them now, trying to get the right light for their cameras!"

They played the license-plate game, of course--Ben always did--with disappointing results, only thirty-one (at one point Ben was heard to mutter, "Goddam New Mexico cars!"). They also ate well, except for Jack's cold, hard, overcooked Louisiana catfish the first night out and a dreadful Polynesian buffet in Alamogordo; otherwise they ate a great deal of very good Mexican food and a lot of cheeseburgers.

Their itinerary was altered somewhat when Ben's Buick 8 broke down just outside of Fort Stockton on their way from Carlsbad to San Angelo. They limped into town to the Buick dealership and spent most of the morning and a good part of the afternoon waiting in the showroom for it to be repaired. When it was finally ready, they took off and got a few miles out of town when it broke down again. They limped back, put the car back in the garage, and checked into a motel. It was late the next morning before they got the car, and they drove straight through to Jasper, arriving well past midnight, whiling away a good portion of the time composing an epic of sorts in terza rima. As the remaining fragments reveal, the world may rejoice that it was composed well after dark and, therefore, Johnny could not see to write it down.

It was on this trip that Johnny began his career as the Keeper of the Official Trip Book, recording images, snatches of conversation, quotable quotes, and other assorted impressions. A sampling of what he recorded provides some idea of the tone of the trip, best described, perhaps, as zany; the quotations, unless otherwise noted, are Ben's:

"I wouldn't want to eat breakfast with Truth; maybe supper."

* * *

On morning strawberries: "O that looks good; I wish I hadn't seen that."

* * *

To a waitress taking up the plates at the Holiday Inn: "I'm getting half of his hushpuppy—then I'll let you have it."

* * *

On one of Duncan Eaves' ideas about slavery: "They were happy in the cottonfields—not to mention Duncan's mother's kitchen, where they were utterly blissful."

* * *

In reference to a line from a poem by Leon Stokesbury: Kimpel last saw Porky Pig 13 years, 9 months and 3 days ago. August 24, 1961. Cloudy but not raining. Subject was boarding plane in Little Rock for Miami. Subject had no pants on—bow tie, purple coat, Che Guevara hat. Porky lives. Kimpel out to watch planes take off, he says. Claims to have known P.P. only by reputation.

* * *

"Dr. Kimpel, who would you least like to meet in that mountain pass—Apaches, Chinese, or French Symbolists?"

"French Symbolists, of course."

"Why?"

"They brought about the modern tradition, and you know the result of that."

"No. What?"

"Us. People making a pilgrimage to the grave of a pornographer. That would never have happened had it not been for Mallarme."

* * *

On defective audio equipment in Carlsbad Cavern: "Please whack your listening device on a large rock before handing it to the attendant."

* * *

Why Ben would never have made it as a big-time capitalist: "I'd ask them if they wanted some Pepsi, and if they did I'd sell it to them."

* * *

Johnny: "Why did you go see 'Journey to the Center of the Earth' in New Zealand?"

Ben: "Because it was there."

* * *

Jack's Mountain Brook Trout Revenge: "Take that, Louisiana catfish!"

* * *

"Dr. Kimpel, was Jesus Christ the greatest Irishman of them all?"
"Well, he was an Irishman; I don't know if he was any greater than James Joyce."

* * *

Jack, after five or six days: "I feel like a skin stretched around four hundred Mexican dinners."

* * *

On seeing a sign reading 'You are now entering the air base' late in the evening after driving from Carlsbad and getting lost trying to find White Sands: "I don't want to enter the air base!"

* * *

One of several original limericks:
"There once was a writer named Lawrence
Whose 'hateds' would gush out in torrents.
He loathed high society
And middle-class piety.
Machines were his special abhorrence."

* * *

Never having been to a Stuckey's, Ben proves to be a latter-day Will Rogers: "I never met a man I didn't like at Stuckey's."

* * *

Jack's pilot for a TV mystery series:

"Sheriff, you know that body we found outside 'La Cocina' early this morning?"

"Yeah, Buzzwheat, what'd the autopsy turn up?"

"Well, sheriff ... somethin' mighty strange."

"I ain't got time for guessin' games, Buzzwheat—what turned up?"

"Well, sheriff, you know how the body's eighty percent water?"

"Yeah, I know how the body's eighty percent water—I know exactly how the body's eighty percent water! Now get on with it, man!"

"Well, sheriff, this body wasn't no eighty percent water; coroner said--and swore he'd never seen nothin' like it--this body's eighty percent Mexican dinner!"

* * *

On seeing yet another license plate that they already had: "I wish some of these people from Kansas would go home."

* * *

"Poetry, like Buick mechanics, makes nothing happen."

These snippets of wit and silliness were almost lost to the world when the three stopped in Austin for a cheeseburger late at night during the long trek to Jasper. Johnny left his notebook in the restaurant, not realizing he had done so until they were many miles further on. He wrote the restaurant as soon as he got home, and about a month later, the notebook came in the mail. Ben wrote, "Not that I ever lost faith in the Jack-in-the-Box, but I am relieved so much wit and wisdom will not be wasted. I dug up one more line [of the terza rima epic]: 'Like red-necked mothers waiting for a wall.' But see no chance of restoring the mutilated masterpiece." The line represents a conflation of the titles of two country songs they heard in a bar in Santa Fe.

In addition to visiting Glacier National Park, the Black Hills, and Isle Royal later that summer, Ben left in September for his trip to China; however, confirmation that he was by no means tired of traveling and that he had enjoyed the trip with Jack and Johnny came in January 1976, when we received the following letters, the first written on stationery from the Hotel St. Francis in San Francisco and dated January 6:

Your friendly travel agent, at leisure to contemplate road maps, suggests the following itinerary:

1)   Sunday May 16 ? To Amarillo—special welcome-aboard catfish dinner

2)   Santa Fe—Mexican dinner at Hotel La Fonda, afternoon at leisure to re-explore that quaint & exotic town

3)   Monument Valley, Utah—Goulding's Trading Post—c. 330 m.

4)   Circle south of lake into Arizona & north again to Zion National Park, Utah

5)   In the park, walking the spectacular scenic trails & observing (perhaps) gila monsters

6)   via Cedar Breaks to Bryce Canyon, breathtaking desert scenery of eroded rocks--Ruby's Inn

7)   to just outside Canyonlands (no accommodations in the park)—via Capitol Reef to Moab

8)   by boat into Canyonlands

9)   by jeep into Canyonlands

10)   via Arches Nat'l Park & Black Canyon of the Gunnison to someplace in central Colorado—Canon City?

11)   via Royal Gorge & Pueblo to fabled Dodge City

12)   via Okla. to Fayetteville, Ark., home of the famed Razorbacks, winners of the Cotton Bowl.

            Ben

January 12, 1976
Dear All,

Hope Susan does go; I'll hold off on reservations till we know.

I am not (quite) omniscient—I have stayed at Goulding's & I got Ruby's Inn from a book on Nat'l Parks (Bryce Canyon lodge still closed in May).

Don't know when I'll stop struggling against my provincial self (which is, indeed, there), but not this year.

            Ben

February 23, 1976
Dear Arkadelphians [=Brothers of Noah's Ark?)--

. . . All reservations heard from except Amarillo. I told them to forget it unless they could unfreeze catfish for four; they must be considering. I have reserved two double rooms at each place; if yours is too cramped, Jack can sleep in mine. Jeep trip to canyons arranged--boat trip appears to cause more trouble.

Ben

The gusto and good humor apparent from these notes were characteristic of all of our trips with Ben, as well as of any time spent in his company. His energy and endurance were phenomenal; he could pack more experience into a day than most of us would consider trying to work into a week. On long days' drives, his playfulness and sense of both fun and adventure never abated; until I was with Ben, I would never have believed that anyone could stay in a good mood all day, every day, for two weeks, but he did, and because he did, we generally did, too.

We did not take a trip with him in 1977 because Johnny had received an NEH summer seminar at CUNY with John Hollander. That summer provided us with a number of motifs that would run through Ben's correspondence for years to come. One had to do with Harold Bloom's theory of the "anxiety of influence" and another with Johnny's reaction to the waiters in a moderately expensive restaurant, Romeo Salta, that Ben had recommended we try.

We missed not having our trip with Ben that year, but in 1978 we went on a mammoth trip through Kansas and Colorado to the Grand Tetons, across to the Black Hills and back to Fayetteville. Jack's second wife, Vicki, went on that one, and a combination of the very long distances and the rather cramped quarters in the car contributed to her developing a rather severe problem with her back by the time we got to South Dakota. We stayed that night at the State Game Lodge (of Teddy Roosevelt fame), and at dinner that night, something extraordinary happened, although it is difficult to say just what it was.

Vicki came to the restaurant in the Lodge for dinner, but she soon excused herself to go lie down. We spoke of taking her to an airport so she could fly home, but she insisted that she would be all right. After she went back to her room, Ben began to apologize to us for having planned such a grueling trip; our protestations that he was in no way to blame only made him more insistent that he was. We had not eaten since noon and were late getting to dinner, and Ben had had several drinks while we were waiting for our meal. He was a little drunk. The combination of his feeling bad about Vicki and his being slightly tipsy put him in a mood we had never seen before and never saw again. He berated himself for ten or fifteen minutes and in the process came as close to becoming maudlin as Ben ever could. When he finally stopped, we finished our meal in high spirits, but something was different. Johnny and Jack and I all felt it, and I think Ben did, too. He had showed us a side of himself that he rarely revealed, and it had effected some kind of breakthrough in our relationship. We all look back on that evening as a turning point of sorts; afterwards, we were much more at ease with Ben than before, and the intimacy that characterized the remaining years of our friendship with him began.

CHAPTER NINE

Johnny's correspondence with Ben picked up significantly following the summer of 1978. Much of what Ben was responding to in the following letters--all sorts of questions, quizzes, and the like--is lost, although some of it is self-evident; however, for their wit, their insight into his playful spirit, and their testimony to his unique warmth I reproduce them here, grouped as nearly chronologically as possible. I have added notes of explanation where I could.

1978

[Johnny, having coerced Ben into passing through a corner of Iowa--a state Johnny had not been in before--on our return from the Black Hills, proclaimed himself "a Hawkeye till I die." One of the motifs on our 1976 trip had grown out of a combination of a phrase—"900 pounds of man-eating terror"—used to tout a movie about a killer bear—*Grizzly* I think it was called—which was playing virtually everywhere on our route and a game devised by our mutual friend Larry Johnson. It occasioned a seemingly endless stream of such exchanges as "a movie about killer brooms": Straws; "a movie about killer blackbirds": Daws, and so on, and a lot of "so many somethings of man-something something." Jack was living in Fayetteville, where he had returned to graduate school in the fall of 1977.]

Dear Hawkeye and spouse--

I was able to explain to Jack "what Americans want" as soon as he explained to me *The Other Side of the Mountain.* 14,000 feet of man-warming mush.

I can't imagine *why* you think I wouldn't bribe waiters. I could tell myself that it was for your ultimate good (education); but who knows, I might even enjoy it. As I drift off to sleep, I hear a condescending foreign accent saying, "Excuse me, sir, this is the glass for white wine." Jack says he has no fears, but that you, being upwardly mobile, are vulnerable—

Ben

[Ben disclosed to us that, when he was in Europe during the war, he had filled out absentee ballots for a whole group of service men who didn't care who won the presidential election and told him to cast their votes for whomever he pleased.]

Dear Johnny--

Of course I couldn't get along without you. I'd have to give up dreaming of that condescending waiter. If this be original sin . As for ballot boxes, my role was more like that of the League of Women Voters except that I was even more helpful. Instead of just driving people to the polls, I saved them all the trouble.

I have never tripped a Wampus Cat. It would, perhaps, be rash to say I never will, but I can hope.

But I do admire your discovery about Venus & Adonis-very much. It's much closer than the refrigerator. Congratulations on a major break-through.   Ben

[Ben sometimes answered Johnny's letters by writing on the letter and sending it back, as he did with the following. The camel refers to a little song that Ben made up on our trip to Utah in 1976:

Oh, it's hard to tell a camel from a cobra;
Both are trochees, both beginning with a c.
It is hard when you are drunk or when you're sob'rer,
It is hard for you and also hard for me.
But though life may often seem confused and hectic,
One can always tell the real thing from the sham;
For a cobra always stays acatalectic,
While a camel's friends may sometimes call him Cam.] .

Johnny: Have we ever seen a Delaware license plate on our trips?

Ben: One Delaware car has ventured west of the Alleghenies. It was in Yosemite in 1972. I hope it got home safely--it has not been seen since. Tell Dennis (Jackson) the next time we go west, he'll have to be the second adventurous soul & accompany us in his car. There is a Vermont car in the parking lot of the Communications Center—every day.

[Johnny tells something he has already told.]

Ben: Your mind is busy with too many things--seek the one thing needful.

Johnny: Just now I'm perusing a large number of texts for the verbal germ of that elaborate salt and pepper shaker we saw at dinner a few miles from Ruby's Inn.

Ben: Right on. Surely Donne has something.

Johnny: You write, "I have never tripped a Wampus Cat." But can you be sure? Are you always able to recognize a Wampus Cat when you see one? If not, how can you know that some of those things you have tripped in your life weren't Wampus Cats? It is, after all, hard to tell a Wampus Cat from a camel, and I know you've tripped a few camels in your day. Isn't it just possible that some (perhaps only one) of those tripped camels were Wampus Cats?

Ben: Don't be silly. Wampus Cats are amphimacers. If one confused them with anything, it would be roller skates. But I've *never* done that.

Ben

Dear Johnny--

(3) Never have I doubted that each contestant for Miss America is a superior being. Why did you think you needed to tell me that?!? Anyway, best regards to Naylene, & I hope folks in Arkadelphia also treat her great. Why wouldn't they? It takes, however, a leap of faith to go from Naylene to the Deity. But faith is not impossible.

(2) I assume LLM is Snow White? or she thinks you are? Ambiguity of the comma. It cannot, however, with that comma, mean that I think you're Snow White. I don't.

(1) I don't know. Ambrose Bierce? Whoever wrote it is as witty as Donne & should have sent it to A. Pope to be verified.

Ben

[Ben had said, regarding a sonnet of Johnny's beginning "Television in Texas . . . ,"that an iambic line could not begin with two reversed feet; I told Johnny to ask him about "Let me not to the marriage of true minds." Johnny had begun studying Latin and, with a very meagre vocabulary to work with, was playing around with cases.)

Dear (?) Johnny--

So now, not content with your own probing questions, you send spies around to probe.

$1/200,000,000 = .0000000005\%$ (I think). No wonder they considered me negligible in their calculation. But to be accurate the figures are $.90\%$ and $.9999999999\%$.

How can I be responsible for the metrical deficiencies of mere popular playwrights?

The one thing needful is the spirit (viewless wings) of poesy.

Being, like Rabelais, a hero up to the scaffold exclusively, I'd teach the *Volsungasaga*. You can tell that to Camus.

The poet's poet gives a poet to the poet??? Nonsense.

But I do want to know who wrote "Lose not a button." Great stuff.

Count Orso was a decidedly *inferior* being.

With aid from the original, I'd guess Goethe. I don't think it's an equation. The not's cancel neatly, but the "others" are on one side only. -Ben

Dear Inquisitor--

1. Because her husband will have the Chinks, of course.

2. I do not like "soil your exquisite ear."

3. Is "the poet's poet gives the poet a poet" any better?

4. You quoted--how can you forget?--a beautiful short poem, by someone in the 19th cent. (so it's not by you), beginning "Lose not a button"--as a test.

5. I hope you have exciting adventures, but please try not to have them in Christian Athletics. In Athletics, if you must. In Christian somethings, OK. Not both.

6. I can only assume that the Nazis disliked Beethoven because he was American--same reason they dislike Christ and Athletics.

7. The painting, of course, is *Les Saltimbanques*. But "who is the painted"? What does that mean? A Saltimbanque. For his name, you might write Picasso if he weren't dead.

8. I am eagerly looking forward to the Razorback basketball games, especially since I'm not watching the Long Search for my kicks. I did watch The Mayor of Q. First rate.

Now, to keep you off my back for a while, a quiz for you, the student of Latin. I won't answer another question till you tell me the meter of the Goethe poem (it is verified, but not exactly as Pope would have verified it).

Ben

"copain" is closer to "pal" than "ami"

[On our 1976 trip, we found in restaurants, mainly in Utah, little booklets by one Dan Valentine filled with schmaltzy essays using the formula title "What is a _ ?"]

Petit copain--

Well (as someone said to a colleague during a Dept. meeting), you've disgraced yourself again! (1) I asked for a specific name, and you can be sure (I being notoriously fair-minded) that it's a well-known one--as a matter of fact, gave its name to a famous school of poets; (2) all students of Latin know that dactylic hexameter can have spondees in feet 1, 2, 3, &/or 4, & *must* have a spondee or trochee in foot 6; but neither they nor trochaic lines can be catalectic in the middle.

Nevertheless, I will answer (1) Un irlondais (we don't capitalize French adjs., even national ones) est un sourire. As on Easter, 1916. I have an Irishman on my face right now.

(2) I have twice this fall run from my house yelling, "The season is ruined!" And now they say we may lose the son of a bitch who ruined it!

(3) Un homme de Bali est forcement un irlondais, parcequ'il est un sourire.

(4) Of course I didn't just know that line. Why should I remember lines out of a poet [Shakespeare] who doesn't even know metrics?

(5) Didn't you write your thesis on that medieval mystic Johannes Cheeverius? Of course you're a candidate. Please forward offprints of medieval scholarly articles & a letter from your thesis director on your medieval scholarship.

(6) May? or haven't you yet corrected OBU's off-beat schedule?

(7) I prefer "Herd melodies are sweet" to "The quality of mercy." Even more concise, & closer to the original.

(8) How could you forget "Lose not a button"? You've disgraced yourself again.

(9) Please try to make your questions as American as possible. No more French painters in German poems.

(10) How can I admire Sunday P.M. on the Big Basin? Is it American?

(11) I do not think "Desert Places" is the greatest French Symbolist poem. Frost is American. You slander him. I do often hear that voice, but I always assumed Satan was speaking.

Ben

[Ben had been in New York City interviewing candidates for a position at the University at the MLA convention over the Christmas holidays, and Johnny had recommended to him one of our favorite restaurants in Greenwich Village. Ben had not gone because, he said, it was too far from his hotel, and Johnny had upbraided him for being unwilling to walk so far "for friendship." We were planning a trip for the summer of 1979, possibly to the east coast.)

Dear Johnny--

We haven't quite picked our medievalist, but I interviewed some of them; queried all of them on Cheeverius, & they were all fully informed. One girl is working on his lesser-known Latin treatises. Seems he was struggling against being overwhelmed by Johannis P. Marquanda--so much for the antediluvian age. Perhaps even Bloom can err?

50 whole blocks just for friendship!! Farthest I got from Central Park was N.Y. Public.

Surely I didn't say anything about my reservations on The Doors of Perception. I haven't read it. Perhaps that was my reservation?

In August I plan to be in New Haven. If you & Susan get that far, I'll show you Vt. & N.H., complete with license plates.

I knew it mattered. Have I ever muttered? NO.

Ben

[John Calhoun had been in graduate school with us and had a wonderful and wicked wit in which Ben and the rest of us took great delight; he had once proposed a sexual reading of Ben's favorite religious lyric, George Herbert's "Love III," after which Ben shook his head and said rather sadly, "I'm not sure I can thank you for that." Ben was teaching a course in the contemporary British and American novel in the spring of 1979.]

Dear Johnny--

I agree--Susan, Jack, Johnny can all write. Which best? Quien sabe?

12 1/4 blocks--13 1/2 in good weather [how far he would walk for friendship].

"Continental" was a typist's error--like your grammatical sins--for "contemporary." Shall I design a syllabus for continental novel? You'll have read them all.

I will *not* try to satisfy my curiosity about how anyone could get John Calhoun & me confused. I don't want to know. I'm afraid to know.

I think I'll really have leisure to chase the elusive N.H. license plate in its native haunts.

My only reservation about *On the Road* is that *that* boy, unlike Susan, Jack, Johnny, *can't* write--very often, only when his characters are stoned, only briefly.

All questions, as always, answered.

Ben

Dear Johnny--

My doctor has warned me often against extremism—not that he ever needed to. I am a middle-of-every-reader, as you know. OK except when you have to pass.

If you can get your provincial little pals to collect only $5000, I'll be glad to insult them individually or as a group. I'll even do my imitation of a waiter at Romeo Salta's. Arkansas has everything right within its own borders.

One date in early August is as good as another, as long as it includes a Sunday (Yale library closed). You've touched my heart with those 14 blocks, & I'll just as big-heartedly sacrifice 2 or 3 days of Pound work.

Surely that passage on the eye (if you haven't forgotten it) is Thomas Mann?

1. Swann's Way
2. The Counterfeiters
3. The Plague
4. Zorba the Greek

5. The Good Soldier Schweik
Just don't write *me* a nasty letter.
Ben
[For financial reasons, we had to cancel our proposed trip to the east coast.]

Dear Johnny--

Since you are unwilling to mortgage your financial future, I reduce my walk to 6 blocks, in spring & fall, 3 in summer, & 1 in winter.

I am disappointed. Condemned to nothing but Pound! But I can live with it. Would Hot Springs be budgetarily possible? I should have a week-end in May to get out from under my rock--briefly.

Surely *all* the writers in my course have been called by *someone* the only American writer of genius? John Hollander said it of James Michener? I know J.M. is not in my course, but did J.H. know it? No. Or J.H. said it of J.H.?
Ben

Dear Johnny--

After my intuitive triumph on Mann, I'm going to rest on my laurels & pretend I didn't notice your latest quotations.

I register appreciation of your walk in the cold, & add 2 blocks to my estimate--on a nice spring or fall day.

Congratulations to Kansas!

Randall J. should have warned Bloom not to be a Bloomitt. My brother-in-law takes *Sports Illustrated*. I have put in my overnight bag, in preparation for my next trip to Fort Smith, the date Feb. 26, 1979.

I am *not* a Kimpelitt.
Ben

October 3, 1979
Dear Johnny--

Business: Prospects are quite good. He should write me between November and February [we had a student interested in applying to Fayetteville for a graduate assistantship in English for the fall of 1980.]

Pleasure: I have, of course, become TOO GOOD. But you knew that. Mainly, I have nothing to say except (1) I have read *Garp* (and CM); (2) I wish you and Susan would come to Fayetteville.

Sincerely,

Dr. Ben Drew Kimpel, Pound Scholar

October 22, 1979

THIS IS NOT A LETTER

The broader of my two day beds is 39" wide. They could be put together, but the middleman might fall through. I also have a comfortable sofa, & Gene could be moved when the living room is no longer in use. You now have the evidence.

[Johnny sent Ben a form with the following note: "Play like a Martian has landed in Siloam Springs. He takes a bus to Fayetteville and comes to your office. He tells you that he has it on good authority from Ray Bradbury that you can help him understand what the earth and earthlings have been by filling out a certain form he has brought with him. Being the helpful man you are, you consent to fill out the form. You ask for a few days to ponder. He grants you the few days and tells you to mail the form to Johnny Wink, with whom he plans to spend several weeks.

FORM: For each category choose five earthly productions which, in your view, represent the best earthlings have been able to do in that area." Ben filled out the form as follows.]

Musical Compositions (non-literary)

1. Mozart, Clarinet Concerto
2. " Piano " 27
3. " Piano " 25
4. " Piano " 27
5. " Piano " 27

Musical Compositions (literary)

1. *Marriage of Figaro*
2. *Magic Flute*
3. *Don Giovanni*
4. *Cosi Fan Tutte*
5. *Boris Godonov*

Paintings

1. Rembrandt, Self-Portrait
2. " "
3. " "

4.   "   "

5.   "   "

Sculptures

1.   Michelangelo, Florence Pietà

2.   "   "   Medici Tombs

3.   "   Rome Pietà

4.   "   " Moses

5.   "   " David

Photographs

After a careful study of my bedroom wall, I can't prefer one to another.

Movies

1.   *Beau Geste*

2.   *Robin Hood*

3.   *The Thief of Bagdad*

4.   *The Mark of Zorro*

5.   *42nd Street*

Religious, Mythical Documents

1.   Jonah

2.   Matthew

3.   Ruth

4.   Tao te Ching

5.   *The Man Who Died*

Lyric Poems

1.   The Garden

2.   To His Coy Mistress

3.   Love III

4.   The Ecstasy

5.   Definition of Love

Narrative Poems

1.   *Iliad*

2.   *Odyssey*

3.   *Paradise Lost*

4.   *Don Juan*

5.   *Beowulf*

Plays

    1.   *Lear*

    2.   *Hamlet*

    3.   *Tempest*

    4.   *Measure for Measure*

    5.   *Midsummer Night's Dream*

Novels

    1.   *Brothers Karamazov*

    2.   *War & Peace*

    3.   *Possessed*

    4.   *Crime & Punishment*

    5.   *Ulysses*

Essays

    1.   Montaigne, Experience

    2.   "   On Husbanding the Will

    3.   "   Raymond Sebond

    4.   "   On Cripples

    5.   "   On Cannibals

Histories

    1.   *Decline & Fall of the Roman Empire*

The rest are too far behind

Literary Works That Fall Into None of the Above Categories

    1.   *In Praise of Folly*

    2.   *Gargantua & Pantagruel*

    3.   *D[?] of the Gods*

    4.   *Misfortune of Elphin*

    5.   *Larrengro [?]*

Edifices

    1.   Cathedral, Reims

    2.   "   Chartres

    3.   "   Paris

    4.   "   Amiens

    5.   "   Salisbury

Ideals

    1.   Negative Capability
    2.   Tolerance
    3.   Independence
    4.   Humor
    5.   Kindness with Discrimination

Scientific Concepts

    1.   Gravity
    2.   Levity
    3.   Influence of Anxiety
    4.   Entropy
    5.   Uncertainty

[To this Ben added, "My list, you understand, is propaganda, designed to make him love, not understand, us. If I wanted him to understand, I'd list *Mein Kampf*, Genesis, Horatio Alger, *How to Win Friends and Influence People*, and selected speeches by Bob Hope, Khomeini, Billy Graham, and St. Paul."]

Oct. 29, 1979
Dear Johnny & Susan--
        This *is* a letter.
        I'll write or talk to any wife I please about courtesans--even about her husband's courtesans. Don't try to terrorize me.
        I didn't really think *Garp* resembled any cat's meow I've ever heard, but then I'm not a connoisseur of meows. I did enjoy it--really a good deal. Not only because (like *A Separate Peace*) it's set at my old prep school. Mainly because Garp was so nice.
        It would be possible--easy--for me to lodge the two of you. And I'd be glad to. But give me a day's warning so I can get Leo to bring my studio couch back from my office in his truck.
        Rate the following from 1 to 5:
                a.   Joseph Campbell
                b.   margaritas
                c.   Romeo Salta's
                d.   John Hollander
                e.   Your anxiety about the influence of all of the above on you.

[Johnny did spend a weekend with Ben that November, but I did not go. It often happened that, because I viewed weekends as oases during the school year--time to regenerate for another week of teaching, I would forego anything that interfered with their sanctity, even visits with Ben. He made note of my reluctance to go to a number of reunions at various times from 1979 on, the first in December 1979, when he addressed the envelope, usually addressed to both of us, to Mr. Johnny Wink; the following letter was inside.]

Dear Johnny--

N.B. no more Mr. & Mrs. letters till Mrs. comes to Fayetteville.

What countries bound Iran? What countries bound the countries that Iran? If Khomeini has to flee, what is the minimum number of countries he'll have to go through to get asylum in Libya?

Jonah--rare example of the Deity's showing & urging forgiveness.

Ben

Four Seasons-Clift Hotel, San Francisco--MLA Convention, 1979
Dear Susan & Johnny--

Job interviews are over--as many desperate Ph.D.'s as always, many of them very good. I talked to one who at 26 is finishing his thesis & has published 3 books & 5 articles, with much more in the works. In F'ville, publication is now essential.

If K. went to Liberia, he would of course fly--too high even to know what countries he was flying over. But he won't go to Liberia. I have eaten (yesterday) a Chinese crab, as well as a good many other good things. Must wait to see exam schedule before final word on Yucatan.

Ben

1980
Dear Professors W & W--

Glad those Baptists finally recognized a good teacher & their own best interests [I received, after five and a half years of teaching part time and full time at Ouachita Baptist, my first full-time contract).

OK, if Khomeini were so rash as not to go by air, he'd have to cross Iraq & Saudi Arabia. Surely you'll let him take a ferry across the Gulf of Aqaba to skip Jordan & especially Israel? Egypt, Libya (where he'd do much better to stay), Niger, Upper Volta (or Mali), & Ivory Coast (or Guinea) to get to Liberia. Why would he want to? I hope he takes a camel. I don't like to play games with people who are too good, though.

I have never been to Tegucigalpa.

My colleagues are already largely rid of aesthetic impulses, but they still don't seem eager either to farm or fight.

Two main reasons for writing:

(1) After telling you this was *definitely* my last year as chairman, I may have to back down.

(2) I think I can arrange to go to Yucatan during exam period, for a little more time than during spring vacation.

Think about it. I've asked Martensen Travel to give us a cost estimate.

Ben

Dear S & J--

You're getting too good with that geography. I don't think I'll play any more. You didn't miss a one.

I never speak in a deeper sense. The crab was cooked by a Chinese.

Should I try to charm or bully the rest of the Dept. into hiring the 26-year-old phenomenon? Which is my style?

I see you've omitted *Elmer Gantry* from your Christian Novel course. *Who* wrote *Month of Sundays*? The last letter I answered ordered me to read Carlos Casteneda; I'd rather take your advice and pick J. Campbell. May do it.

The days off during exam week are only six, a little rushed for Yucatan--& New Orleans? What about Christmas?

February 1980
Dear J & S--
Ben

I hope you point out to some of your colleagues that Khomeini is an authentic saint. Perhaps some of them could get to Liberia.

I have discriminated against only one Central American capital. Surely that's permitted. I have been to (& advise going to) Copan.

Chairmanship still unsettled. When I see you, I'll have to explain what "thrust position" is--we're in it. Too complicated for a letter. I do seem to recall that $500. Was I really so rash? Probably. [Johnny had bet Ben months before that Ben would be the chairman of the English department for another term; Ben, vowing that he absolutely would not serve another term, accepted the bet.]

I have to be back in Little Rock to discuss Humanities the Friday of Spring vacation. That would be short for Yucatan, but time enough for Chicago or Big Bend--or New Orleans or Omaha or Atlanta or Fort Stockton or Kentucky or the Home of the Cowboys. I leave it to you.

Ben

We settled, for reasons I don't remember, on El Paso for our trip. Jack and Ben drove down to Arkadelphia on Friday afternoon; when they arrived, Ben bustled in, red-faced with his usual pre trip excitement. The first thing he did was pull five one hundred-dollar bills out of his wallet and throw them on the kitchen table; he had agreed to continue to serve as chairman. Johnny insisted that he had not been serious, but Ben would have none of it and told us to use the money for our expenses on the trip. He did allow us to pay for some of his expenses as well, but for the most part it was for Johnny and Jack and me. We sat for a couple of hours at the kitchen table listening to Ben tell us about "thrust position"--part of the jargon connected with the University's campaign to achieve "eminence" or "national prominence" or some such phrase--and then left for Little Rock, where we took a flight to El Paso.

We arrived at dusk; the lights of El Paso and Juarez were glittering in the clear desert air, and the star on Franklin Mountain was illuminated--normally lit only during the Christmas season, it continued to glow until the hostages being held in Iran had been freed. We checked into a Holiday Inn in downtown El Paso and, during the next four days and five nights, managed to find the very best restaurants in El Paso, Juarez, and Old Mesilla, New Mexico; it turned out to be the best "eating" trip we ever had. When we flew back to Little Rock on Wednesday, we drove directly to Hot Springs and spent that night at the Arlington and had a very good dinner at the Hamilton House. The following night we spent in Arkadelphia, where I prepared our evening meal. Jack and Ben returned to Fayetteville early Friday.

Johnny, as the Keeper of the Official Trip Book, recorded the following dialogues with and comments made by Ben:

"Ben, if a man put a gun to your head and told you to choose between wearing either a panther suit or a t-shirt that said 'Voulez-vous fuck' on the front for the rest of your life, what would you do?"

"I'd say, 'Pull that trigger.'"

* * *

"We had that glory, at least. On my deathbed I'll say, 'I was once in thrust position.'"

* * *

"Ben, I think you have plenty of that one (charity)."
"No, none of us has enough of that one."

* * *

"The first thing I find compelling about people—and the one I don't feel guilty about--is that they should be kind. The second thing is that should have fast minds—because I get bored. The third is that they should be able to do something: write a poem or make a cup of coffee." ·

[In May 1980 I accompanied four OBU graduates on a two-week trip to England and Germany--my first visit to Europe. Johnny had been teaching a course in the Christian novel that spring and had a number of questions concerning Christianity on his mind, most of which he naturally passed on to Ben. The first letter below is Ben's response to a passage from Flannery O'Connor which Johnny had sent to him.]

Dear Susan,
            Bon voyage
                    Ben
Dear F. O'Connor,
        With the greatest respect, I would like to ask you to reconsider what evidence you have for saying that absence of faith ends in forced-labor camps & gas chambers. It is true that forced-labor camps in Siberia may be said to grow out of an absence of your faith, though the people who established them had a faith of their own. The gas chambers of Germany were not, so far as I know, supported by those who lack all conviction, though the Bavarian Catholics lived comfortably with them & the Pope condoned the government that established them. Both were carrying on the time-honored tradition of Torquemada--the unbelievers must be destroyed. Is not faith

based mainly on the feelings of the human heart, the best of which is sympathy with others? Is not this faith, when detached from tenderness, likely to end in terror? Has it not often done so? Those ages which felt less & saw with the unsentimental eye of acceptance, ma'am, butchered the Albigensians & the Waldensians. Haven't you got it ass-backwards?

B.D. Kimpel
Ph.D.

Dear Johnny--

Are you taking care of yourself in your wife's absence? Are you jealous of her?

A good evaluation of *That Hideous Strength*, but not on my main objection, the wickedness & danger of dividing the world into two groups & then encouraging us to imagine the deserved destruction of one of them.

1. In the sight of God, electric & automatic are not only equal but ultimately identical.

2. Titian

3. Jack lacks the qualities of W.B.--he will never get ahead because he is ahead.

4. Alessandro Manzoni (I'm glad you ended with one good choice. Incidentally, the writer of a genuinely Christian novel).

Ben

Dear J & S--

Yes, I entered a dark wood at 35 & never got out--which, however, means also that I haven't been to hell yet. I'm sure Susan got everything out of the heart of Europe that was in it--perhaps more, as EP's friend Natalie Barney said of life. Of course the permanent (till year after next) chairman of the eminent English Dept. at F'v is interested in any student who could see through *That Hideous Strength*.

You're getting too damn clever, with that line from Manzoni. I'm having breakfast (hotcakes with maple syrup) with Jack tomorrow. We'll gossip about you & decide whether it's worthwhile to be ahead.

Ben

Dear Johnny,

I've been struggling with your question about the tragic sense, but I suppose if I don't answer it till I get it answered to my satisfaction, I never will answer it. First of all, I know nothing about personal immortality. But I do know that I don't feel life to be tragic for lack of assurance about it. There is a strong sense (I wouldn't call it tragic, rather wistful or sad) that· it is a shame that so many things pass away even in this life--feelings, friends, desires, interests. One would like (sometimes) to be able to hold onto more. And it seems to me similarly that one would like (sometimes) to hold onto a feeling that oneself will, in some sense, continue. But then what self? The 12-year-old? The 30-year-old? The "permanent" core of oneself? But where is it? How can one imagine any of one's various selves going on & on forever? How can one want it except momentarily, in pensive mood? And if in the afterlife one is to be so changed that the self can be imagined to endure forever, what is personal about that ossified self? The afterlife will either change us beyond recognition so that what lives on is hardly more recognizably ourselves than what lives on in the synagogue of the ear of corn, or it will fix a self that can't bear itself for more than a few years in a row, or it will be perpetual change, which doesn't sound to me like personal immortality--for where is the person? No, I don't feel that immortality in any sense in which I can understand it is to be desired, though perhaps Someone Else knows better. He may have an offer I can't refuse, though I don't think he'll be as cruel as C. S. Lewis in dividing us into sheep & goats. Surely He can't be nastier than I am, & even in my worst moods I could never, if I could prevent it, make anyone miserable for more than 30 seconds unless I could see that the misery would lead (not just to a higher harmony) but to that person's being ultimately better off. All of this comes to the fact that I can't imagine personal immortality & therefore can't, in any meaningful sense, want it. There is quite enough to do in this life to carry us through our 70-or-so years.

I do find Unamuno moving, as everyone who feels strongly the difference between our reach & our grasp is moving. But the desire for immortality strikes me as only one aspect of the aging of unfulfilled desire, & not the one that interests me most--for instance, achieving some justice (or better, kindness) in society moves me more because I can imagine it better, and because there is perhaps a little bit that we can do to help move an inch closer to it, whereas I can only leave the question of Immortality to--?

At most, we can only try to make ourselves a little more like the person whom, assuming he is to live forever, we could be least unhappy to live with.

Ben

Dear Johnny--

You *do* ask hard questions. Glad we don't have you making out Ph.D. prelims.

Yes, I do feel that a Christian is ~~almost~~ obligated to take a position on sheep & goats similar to C. S. Lewis's--until Christianity becomes entirely symbolic, at any rate. Milton & Dante do, of course, & so did everyone in Europe when they were alive. But a distinction--I have no "spleen" against Milton or Dante or C.S.L. (or so I think, anyway), but I do disagree with them on this point. So must I disagree with all Christians who are real, not symbolic, Christians. But to disagree with someone about a belief which for him was inevitable or inescapable is not very important. With the same belief, Dante, Milton, Browne, Bunyan, Herbert came up with quite different attitudes (Dante's is, for me, rather harsh at times; Milton damns mainly his own sin, pride, which is fair enough; Browne wishes God were as nice as he was) . In any case, as far as others are concerned, we're not called on to do anything about hell & heaven, except perhaps not to gloat. But CSL (in *THS* anyway) carries the same sheep/goat dichotomy into modern life, which puts him in the same category as Catholics & Protestants in Belfast, Jews & Arabs, communists & capitalists, conservative and radical life-stylers, & a host of other undesirables (not in themselves--they may all be very kind people--but in the logic of their moral indignation, a quality of which we have an all-too-rich supply). A Christian is bound to believe that God will reward & punish; he is not bound to jump the gun & give God advice about whom to do what to. The idea that we choose heaven or hell for ourselves seems to me a play on words. We do not choose eternal suffering, though some of the sins we choose, if continued forever, would mean eternal suffering--& some (most middle-class money sins) not. If we've chosen badly, He doesn't need to hold us to it forever. Generally we choose a lot of contradictory things, & at worst He could destroy us. But it's not the effects in the afterlife of a sheep/goats dichotomy that bother me, but the effects in this life. Moral indignation is the feeling that enables us to be cruel & self-righteous at the same time.

Personal mortality, being non-existence, doesn't have to be imagined. I non-existed in 1914; I don't have to imagine it--it's a fact.

My ability to "get in touch" with lots of contrary attitudes? I can try to present them fairly in class, but of course I can't "believe" in them all. I can argue for or against a proposition for educational purposes, but if someone asks me what I think, I must say either "yes," "no," or "I don't know." On the afterlife, I've said, "I don't know." On the people I know or know of, & by extension other people who I must assume are rather like the ones I do know, being either sheep or goats, I say "no."

　　　　Ben

CHAPTER TEN

Paul Valéry maintained that "writers never really finish a piece of work; they only get to the place where they must abandon it." As I approach the point at which I must abandon this work, I am beset by all of the things I have wanted to tell and have not told:

How Ben gave so generously of his time, money, and support to the students at the University--by serving for years, for example, on the executive board of the underground newspaper, *The Grapevine*, by helping organize groups to guard anti-war protesters when they were threatened by violence, by bailing number less students out of jail for almost any offense unless it involved drugs, by teaching off-campus courses, giving lectures, and making himself generally available for both formal and informal gatherings.

How his main objection to marijuana was that people who were smoking it were so boring. "They think they're all being very clever, and they're not."

How he gleefully gave us high fives one night in a motel parking lot when we found a North Dakota license plate.

How he could be wonderfully bawdy--he once contributed to an impromptu song that he and some of his friends were composing the couplet "I wish that all women were statues of Venus,/And I wish that I had a petrified penis," and one of his favorite limericks was "There once was a young man named Dave, / Who kept a dead whore in a cave. / He said, 'I'll admit/I'm a bit of a shit,. / But look at the money I save.'"

How he responded to a young woman when she asked if he had ever drunk champagne from a woman's navel: "No. Should I?"

How infectious and genuine his quiet laugh was when he was really tickled by something.

How he prized and hoarded the tomato juice cocktail that my mother, Cody Wade, used to make. She gave him at least a quart of it every summer for several years, and when we'd take it to him, he would disappear with it, squirreling it away somewhere until we were gone. Late one summer Johnny wrote Ben, "You are the proud owner of a new batch of Cody's tomato juice cocktail, which we will bring when next we come to Fayetteville." Ben sent the letter back with his responses in the margins; he had underlined "when next we come to Fayetteville" and written in large letters, "Be more specific. I want my TJC soon!" Another time when he was trying to get us to set a date for a weekend visit, he wrote, "Of course, I'm not as anxious to see you now that I have my jar of Cody's ever-reliable, ever-delicious tomato juice cocktail." Ben had responded with near-outrage when Johnny suggested that the cocktail made great Bloody Marys: "You don't mix something that good with anything," he said, "not even vodka!" And later he wrote, in an attempt to increase his consignment, "I should think that in future Cody would furnish T.J. cocktail only to one she can be sure won't desecrate it."

How he wanted colors, like tomato juice cocktail, to be vivid and unadulterated. He much preferred bright, pure colors to pastels and detested redbud trees because "they can't make up their minds whether to be pink or purple."

How he valued the friendships of so many different kinds of people. He was really very shy, however, and could not be alone comfortably with other people who happened also to be shy. To enjoy them--and he did enjoy them--he needed at least one other person present, someone uninhibited, someone like Duncan Eaves or Jessie O'Kelly or Johnny Wink. Frequently, with time, he and the other shy one would hit upon a way to be comfortable with each other.

How I never saw him weep.

How clumsily but how dearly he showed his affection. Being hugged and kissed by Ben was like being hugged and kissed by one's affectionate but self-conscious adolescent son.

How, three years after Ben's death and a month before his own, Duncan Eaves was filled with spontaneous joy as he laughed and told me stories about Ben for an hour, and how, when we parted, his eyes brimmed with tears as he said, "A day doesn't pass that I don't think of him."

Hundreds of other images, anecdotes, and testimonies beg to be acknowledged here. Turning them away, I temper my ruthlessness by saying, "Another time."

I saw Ben for the last time in February 1983. In 1979, I had begun taking French at Ouachita and by 1983 had taken every course offered. Needing a break from teaching as well as wanting to perfect my French, I asked for and received a year's leave of absence so I could go to France. I was in Fayetteville on other business for only a day and a half but visited with Ben in his office and invited him to have dinner that night with me and David Strain, with whom I was staying. He accepted. I fried chicken, of course.

I had told him that afternoon about my plans to live in France for a year and asked him what cities--towns, really; I wanted to live in a small place--he might recommend. When he arrived at David's that night, he had several suggestions, but none of them happened to be in the region of France I had my heart set on. When I told him that, for whatever reasons, I would like to live in Burgundy, he thought a minute and said, "There's a perfectly charming town in Burgundy called Beaune--but it may be a little too small."

David dug out his encyclopaedia, and we looked up the population of Beaune--10,000--in 1970. Ben thought that might be all right.

We had dinner and talked for hours about other things. Suddenly Ben said, "Susan, I've been thinking about it--and I think that Beaune is just exactly where you ought to go."

And so, of course, I did.

I didn't leave for France until August 1983, some four months after Ben's death. Throughout the following year, filled as it was with wonderful experiences, I caught myself a hundred times thinking, "I can't wait to tell Ben about this!" He was much on my mind. I wrote the following dream to Johnny in late September 1983: "Ben and: I were sitting at our kitchen table in Arkadelphia talking when the phone rang. It was you. I said, 'Guess who I've got here!' Soon, you and David Strain arrived, and I prepared snails the way I had them the other night for all of us. Ben had been abroad. I think of Ben as being abroad—but then, so am I, and he's not here."

Among the letters that we received from Ben after I had seen him in Fayetteville in February of 1983 are two very brief ones, the first of which arrived early in April. Of course, whether or not the last sentence of the letter had for Ben the significance that, in retrospect, it has had for us. It will always touch my heart.

> Dear J & S--
>
> Is there any valid reason the charming but elusive Mrs. Dr. Wink couldn't get to Little Rock in late April or May to celebrate her departure with old friends? It is essential to visit the city soon.
>
> Ben

In Ben's appointment book for 1983, he had written simply "Johnny" on the weekend of April 25. I don't remember the occasion for which Johnny was planning to be in Fayetteville, but he had asked to stay with Ben. The night that Ben died, Johnny was at a retreat for honors students and did not return home until the following morning. A dear friend had called me from Fayetteville hours after Ben's death on Thursday night; he knew that Johnny was going to be in Fayetteville that weekend and, in case Johnny had been planning to leave Arkadelphia early the next morning, wanted to spare him the shock of arriving to find that Ben had died.

Johnny got home from the retreat around ten o'clock Friday morning, and two hours later, both of us numb with grief, we received our last letter from Ben:

Dear Johnny--

    This letter, plus a smile & an at least tentative promise from Susan to try to make it to Little Rock, will entitle you to a bed/couch/place on the floor next Saturday night.

    Ben

And that was all--one breath more; he had passed forever into memory.

Ben is buried in the Forest Park cemetery in Fort Smith in a plot containing five graves. Balfour and Mattie Crane lie beside each other in the front of the plot; Ben's grave, behind them, is flanked by the grave of his father, Ben Drew Kimpel, to the left and that of his uncle William Carey Crane to the right. More than a century of excellence converges upon the spot.

Ben's great-grandfather William Carey Crane, for whom Ben's uncle was named, had written in 1869, that "the cause of education is ranked by no other one demanding the attention of right minded men. It is connected with every interest of society" (quoted by J. M. Carroll in A History of Texas Baptists, Baptist Standard Publishing Co., Dallas, Texas, 1923, 362). In the expression of such a sentiment, as well as in other respects large and small, William Carey Crane appears to have been not only a physical progenitor of Ben's, but a spiritual and intellectual one as well. The many parallels to Ben's attitudes, habits, and passions can be seen from the following excerpts from J. M. Carroll's book:

> Renewed life came to Baylor with the coming of William Carey Crane as her president in 1863. As the noble, self-sacrificing [George W.] Baines went out, the prince among school presidents came in.
>
> As a scholar Dr. Crane was probably the best equipped college man who had been in Texas. It is doubtful whether any man in Texas has ever surpassed him. In emergencies he could teach everything that was taught in a full college course--all the languages, ancient or modern, all the sciences, or anything else. Numbers of his old students yet living can testify to the truthfulness of this statement.
>
> He had a great library. He was an omnivorous reader. He was an indefatigable worker. The author, who was with him constantly and intimately for five years, never knew him to idle away a single moment. He never loafed. In his dress he was always neat and tidy. He was systematic and orderly in everything. His books and papers always had definite places, and were always in their places. In a moment he could at any time find anything among his books or papers . . . .

As a preacher, Dr. Crane was so very far above the ordinary that he was extraordinary. His sermons were always carefully prepared. They were always orderly, logical and climactic in arrangement. As an impromptu popular speaker he was nothing remarkable, but with a subject previously matured and prepared, he was truly great. . . . The conclusions of his sermons or addresses were almost invariably a brief summing up of all the thoughts he had presented, and this summary was given to the audience like solid shot, with a wonderfully human, appropriate and impressive application. On state occasions he was sometimes possibly too intellectual and stilted for the masses, but in revivals he was best himself as a really warm-hearted, soul-moving gospel preacher. Many scores of his pupils and those of the female department at Baylor were converted under his preaching. He was not a writer of many books, but a writer of many articles for magazines, newspapers, etc. His "Life and Literary Remains of Sam Houston" was probably his greatest book.

Dr. Crane could hardly have been called a pioneer. He was probably fifty years in advance of the times in which he came to Texas. It was hard for him to reach back so far and grasp the hands of the people so as to lead them to higher planes, but he did reach the hands of very many, and all these he did lead to higher and nobler ideals and achievements. The small and poorly equipped Baylor of his day did not furnish opportunities for demonstrating all of his wonderful equipment and talents. He was eminently capable of presiding over any of the best colleges of today. (379-81)

The author will never forget the awfulness of the shock which came to him when, quietly studying in his home in Lampasas, these sad words--too sad for interpretation here--first came to him: "Dr. Crane is dead." For a moment he was almost paralyzed. Though thirty-six years have gone by since that news was received, his grief almost overmasters him as he endeavors to write this record. He had never known Dr. Crane to be sick, but a sudden attack of pneumonia quickly carried him away.

So far as old Baylor at Independence was concerned, Dr. Crane's death was the beginning of the end. The master mind, spirit and personality was gone. For more than twenty years the school had lived, and lived to a great purpose, largely through the transfusion of his own rich blood and the investment of his great life. (524)

... He was a man of the most benevolent and forgiving disposition. He never harbored hatred or sought revenge for wrongs received. Z. N. Morrell, in "Flowers and Fruits," gives this just estimate of his scholarship and personal appearance: "As a scholar, he has but few equals, and his superiors are very scarce. His conversation, his literary addresses and his sermons all show that he is not only a profound scholar, but that he has always been a student, and he is a student still. His mental discipline is of the most rigid character. In person he is of medium height, with compact form, inclined to corpulency."

He was willing to spend and be spent for what he undertook. He estimated that he had sacrificed $40,000 of salary, spent over $5,000 of his own means, and contributed nearly $2,000 from his own purse for the success of Baylor University. He also contributed liberally to other objects. He was not a man to underrate himself, or waive the courtesies he considered his due. To strangers he even seemed egotistic, but few men were more approachable and kind-hearted than he to all with whom he came in contact. Many who wear a meeker look and speak very humbly of themselves, have far more esteem for self and contempt for others than was probably ever cherished by this gifted man and scholar. (531)

The more I have discovered about Ben's forebearers, the more compelling has the image become of Ben as the ultimate receptacle for a legacy of the blood; in him were met the kindness, generosity, intelligence, industry, good nature, integrity, vigor, and wit of at least three generations, and, oh, how well met they were. I doubt we shall ever see his like again.

During one of Ben's leaves of absence, he took a course in modern poetry from Richard Wilbur, to whom he claimed to owe, among other things, his great appreciation for the poetry of Wallace Stevens--Ben was always one to acknowledge his debts. The debts owed to Ben can never be acknowledged, for they continue to mount as his students and his students' students carry on, consciously or not, his splendid legacy.

To Richard Wilbur, one of my teacher's teachers, I too owe a great deal. Not the least of Wilbur's gifts to me is the concluding stanza of his poem "Beowulf," a fitting epigraph to this book, which, like the poem, celebrates a hero who struggled mightily against monsters that threaten the welfare of society; the monsters that Ben fought the most diligently and valiantly were intolerance, cruelty, and cruelty's dam, ignorance. with his death we lost a champion.

He died in his own country a kinless king,
A name heavy with deeds, and mourned as one
Will mourn for the frozen year when it is done.
They buried him next the sea on a thrust of land;
Twelve men rode round his barrow all in a ring,
Singing of him what they could understand.

Made in the USA
Coppell, TX
26 May 2021